THE GRILL MASTER'S BIBLE

Elevate Your Grill Game and Wow Your Guests Each Time with Top Techniques and 1500 Days of Irresistible Recipes that Will Transform Ordinary Cookouts into Exceptional Feasts

Julian Stonewall

Table of Contents

HERE IS YOUR BONUS!

"The Ultimate BBQ Sauce Guide"

We're talking about:

- The science of constructing sauces that will leave your guests craving more.
- The intricacies of rubs and marinades, with a vegetarian alternative.
- Foolproof recipes to elevate any dish, whether it's beef brisket or grilled eggplant.

SCAN HERE TO DOWNLOAD IT

And Unlock the Secret Sauce to BBQ Mastery!

The
ULTIMATE BBQ
SAUCE GUIDE

JULIAN STONEW

Introduction

A Brief History of Grilling

Ah, grilling! It's almost as if it's imprinted in our DNA, a visceral connection dating back to our earliest ancestors. Can't you just picture it? The first prehistoric grill master, furrowed brow under a mop of unkempt hair, clumsily harnessing the power of fire. Suddenly, it was more than just about keeping the prowling beasts at bay. They realized that fire was an ally in transforming their hard-won spoils of the hunt into more digestible, flavorful delights.

Our grilling lineage is evidenced in archaeological excavations from the Middle Stone Age, where we see the remnants of primitive hearths, charred bones, and basic grilling tools that speak of humanity's culinary coming of age.

In ancient Greece, grilling wasn't merely a way to cook dinner—it was a social event, an excuse to make merry and honor the gods. And not just any god, mind you, but Priapus—the god of barbecues, no less! This tradition later spread to the Romans, lending a touch of nobility to their grand feasts.

In medieval Europe, grilling graduated to a new level of sophistication with spit-roasting. Yes, it was labor-intensive, but the end result, a succulent, evenly cooked meat, was worth every bit of effort. A medieval version of showing off, if you will, reserved for celebrations that demanded grand gestures of abundance.

Meanwhile, thousands of miles across the Atlantic, the indigenous people of the Caribbean were nurturing their own grilling traditions, completely unbeknownst to their European counterparts. The first taste of 'barbacoa,' slow-cooked meat over a wooden platform, its flavor infused with a smoky essence that we now associate with quintessential barbecue.

Asia, of course, was not to be left behind. For instance, in the lively neighborhoods of Korea and Japan, the grill has always been more than just a cooking device. With their tabletop grills, Korean 'gogigui' turns the act of cooking into an engaging, communal affair that sparks laughter, conversation, and a shared gastronomic experience.

Here we are now, in the 21st century, where grilling isn't just a way to cook—it's an experience, a ritual that signals warm summer days, family reunions, and cheerful sharing. We've come a long way from our primitive ancestors, trading their rudimentary tools for sleek, high-tech models that range from portable camping varieties to those that could pass off as a professional kitchen fixture.

Yet, the essence of grilling has remained unchanging throughout the millennia—it's a social affair, a tradition that brings people together. Every time we fire up our grills, we're connecting with our ancestors, partaking in a ritual that's as old as civilization itself.

Isn't it fascinating how grilling, in its many forms, has seared itself into our global culinary traditions, cutting across cultures and geographies? As we probe further into the art and science of grilling, remember, whether you're a novice or an experienced pit master, this book is here to arm you with the knowledge and finesse to elevate your grilling game. So, are you ready to turn up the heat?

The Basics

Different Types of Grills

Embarking on the rewarding journey of grilling? Well, let me tell you, my friend, the choices you have at your fingertips are as varied and exciting as the smoky, sizzling delicacies you're about to create. Understanding the personalities of different types of grills is, as we love to say, part of the essential 'mise en place' of this grilling adventure. From the conventional charm of charcoal grills to the convenience of gas models, each type has its own set of rewards and challenges.

Charcoal grills, the classic choice for many grilling aficionados. They are like that rustic, old-school rock band that never goes out of style. Their main draw? That unmistakable, authentic smoky flavor that sets the tone for a memorable cookout. Imagine biting into a steak or burger seared over charcoal, and you'll understand what we mean. The coals not only cook your food but also artfully create a divine crust. There is a flip side, though. Charcoal grills require time to reach the optimal heat and controlling that temperature can be difficult, especially for beginners.

The gas grill is the quick-draw artist of the grill world. Using either propane or natural gas, these machines of convenience heat up in a snap, often clocking under ten minutes. They're the ever-reliable sous-chef in your grilling kitchen, offering easily adjustable, consistent heat. Multiple cooking zones at different temperatures? Check. Perfect for juggling a diverse menu. However, while convenient, they lack some of the smoky flavor of their charcoal cousins.

The compact and controlled character of electric grills makes them perfect for those grappling with space restrictions or regulations around open flames - think apartments or condos. Easy to use, quick to heat, and with straightforward temperature control, they're a pretty great ally to have. But let's face it, without an actual flame, you might find the classic grilled flavor playing a bit hard to get.

And then, we have the travel-friendly portable grills. Whether you're planning a sun-kissed beach cookout, an adventure-filled camping trip, or a heart-pounding tailgate party, these little troopers won't let you down. Their ace? They come in all fuel types - charcoal, gas, and electric. While their cooking space might be on the smaller side, they more than make up for it with their adaptability and portability.

If the deep, smoky flavor of slow-cooked meat sets your heart racing, then meet your match: smokers. These specialists are designed to cook over longer periods, using low heat and lots of smoke, perfect for BBQ staples like ribs or brisket. But with great flavor comes great responsibility - managing the long cooking times and maintaining a steady temperature can be a bit of a challenge.

There is no "one grill to rule them all" in the world of grilling.' It's a spectrum of preferences and needs, a balance of flavor and budget, of spatial considerations, and your unique grilling style. Each type of grill holds the promise of a different journey, each one laden with its own set of flavors, experiences, and delicious discoveries.

Key Factors When Choosing a Grill

The act of selecting the ideal grill is a nuanced process, an intensely personal decision influenced by various pivotal considerations. A grill is far from being a mere appliance: it's an investment in a lifestyle.

So, let's delve into these factors you should consider.

Fuel Type

The initial and arguably, one of the most crucial considerations is the fuel type. Your grill's lifeblood, the fuel, can significantly influence the cooking process and the resulting flavor. The classic charcoal grill is a purist's delight, generating high heat and the much-coveted smoky flavor, albeit with a slower cooking time. Gas grills, whether propane or natural, offer the gift of convenience and precision in temperature control. However, the trade-off might be a slightly subdued smoky flavor profile. For the urban dwellers confined by open flame restrictions, an electric grill can be the ideal choice. Smoker grills, the custodians of slow cooking, use low heat to create a deep, smoky flavor that is nothing short of tantalizing.

Size

Size is the next consideration. Consider the grill's size based on the number of people you typically cook for and your available space. A compact grill may work for small families and tight spaces, but larger groups will likely need a larger, more substantial grill. Bear in mind, a larger grill equates to higher fuel consumption and potentially lengthier cleaning times.

Heat

Heat output, as represented in BTUs (British Thermal Units) for gas grills, is another critical factor. However, high BTUs are not a standalone indicator of the grill's prowess in preheating or cooking. Consider also the grill's size, its design, and its efficiency in heat retention and distribution.

Features

As you venture deeper into your grill selection process, look for features that mirror your unique grilling style. Additional features like side burners, warming racks, rotisserie burners, built-in temperature gauges, and tool hooks can significantly elevate your grilling experience. A multi-burner grill might prove handy for creating different heat zones for diverse food items.

Material and Build Quality

The grill's construction and the quality of materials used are vital considerations as well. Premium materials such as cast iron or stainless steel not only promise a longer life for your grill but also ensure superior heat retention. In addition, while cast iron retains heat superbly and delivers striking grill marks, stainless steel grates are known for their durability and ease of cleaning.

Price

While price inevitably plays a significant role in your decision, it's crucial to perceive your grill as a long-term investment rather than a one-off purchase. Often, a heftier price tag is an indicator of longer durability and superior performance.

Ease of Cleaning

Your grill should not turn into an arduous task post the grilling pleasure. Hence, consider ease of cleaning. Grills equipped with features like removable ash catchers and grease trays are typically easier to clean and maintain.

Brands and Reviews

Finally, remember to pay heed to brand reputations and customer reviews: they provide a useful window into performance and durability. User feedback can offer invaluable insights into how the grill fares over time and under different conditions.

Choosing a grill is like choosing a companion for your culinary adventures. Consider all of your options carefully, be patient, and remember - the right grill will be worth the effort.

Essential Grilling Tools and Utensils

In the culinary arts, grilling stands as an enticing blend of precision, skill, and creativity, each component reliant not only on the source of heat but the right arsenal of tools. The right tools can make the difference between a mediocre meal and a grilled masterpiece. Here are the essential grilling tools and utensils that every aspiring grill master should have in their arsenal:

1. Grill Tongs

A fundamental tool in the hands of every grill artist is a pair of grill tongs. These are your trusted allies in flipping steaks, turning sausages, and moving items around the grill. Opt for long and robust tongs, providing a firm grip without exerting undue pressure on your hand.

2. Spatula

A heavy-duty spatula is crucial for flipping burgers or delicate items like fish fillets. Choose one with a long handle to protect your hands from heat and a strong, thin edge to ensure smooth maneuvering under the food.

3. Grill Fork

A grill fork, another key tool, assists in flipping, shifting, and testing the doneness of food items. Search for a fork equipped with long and sturdy tines, capable of handling substantial chunks of meat.

4. Grill Brush

Maintaining a clean grill is essential, and a good grill brush is key to achieving this. Key traits to look for include a long handle and durable, stiff bristles. Some brushes feature an attached scraper, a useful ally in combating stubborn grill residues.

5. Meat Thermometer

Ensuring your food attains a safe and optimal internal temperature calls for a meat thermometer. Digital versions tend to deliver the highest accuracy and readability. Guesswork has no place in grilling!

6. Basting Brush

You can use a basting brush to add sauces and marinades to your meal as it cooks. Opt for one with silicone bristles as they're easy to clean and won't leave bristles behind on your food.

7. Grill Gloves

Safety holds paramount importance in grilling. Grill gloves, fashioned from high-temperature-resistant materials like leather or aramid fibers, shield your hands from the grill's searing heat, be it while adjusting coals, handling hot utensils, or maneuvering food.

8. Grill Basket

A grill basket is a nifty accessory for grilling smaller items prone to slip through the grill grates, like vegetables or fish. This tool offers the freedom to flip these small foods without worrying about losing them to the flames.

9. Skewers

Skewers, ideal for assembling kebabs or grilling bite-sized pieces of meat or vegetables, come in reusable metal varieties or disposable wooden ones. If opting for the latter, pre-soak them in water to prevent charring.

10. Chimney Starter

For charcoal grill enthusiasts, a chimney starter stands as a vital tool. This device allows quick, even heating of coals sans the need for lighter fluid, lending your food a clean, unadulterated flavor.

11. Smoking Chips: How to Choose the Right Wood

An honorable mention in the grill master's tool kit goes to smoking chips, particularly for those seeking to infuse their food with a tantalizing smoky flavor. Recognize that all woods are not alike; different varieties impart distinct flavors and pair more harmoniously with certain foods.

Applewood, for instance, offers a sweet, fruity smoke ideal for poultry, pork, fish, and even cheese. In contrast, mesquite delivers a robust, earthy flavor suitable for most red meats, though its strong flavor warrants cautious use. Hickory stands as a versatile option, generating a bold flavor that harmoniously complements almost all meats, especially pork and beef.

Similar to applewood, cherrywood creates a sweet, fruity smoke perfect for poultry, and when combined with hickory, it helps balance the latter's potent flavor. Oak, with its moderate smoky flavor, excels with larger cuts of meat requiring extended smoking periods.

Arming yourself with these quintessential grilling tools and utensils, you'll stand prepared to tackle any grilling challenge. Quality tools not only enhance your grilling experience but also influence the flavor outcome positively. In the world of grilling, these tools are your investment for a lifetime.

Proper Care and Maintenance of Your Equipment

Maintaining your grill is an essential part of ensuring its longevity and the quality of your cooking. Attending to your grill's maintenance needs not only guarantees its durability but also preserves the authentic flavors of your grilled creations. Here, we will look at cleaning techniques, storage tips, and safety checks vital for the upkeep of your grilling gear.

1. Cleaning Techniques

Foremost, cleanliness in grilling is a prerequisite for impeccable grilling results. Lingering grease and food remnants can instigate flare-ups, potentially causing uneven cooking or, worse, hazardous fires. Here are a few cleaning procedures to ensure the best grilling results:

The grill grates require regular care. Post grilling, while the grill retains warmth, a stiff wire brush will effectively remove food debris from the grates. Every couple of months, commit to a more thorough cleaning by detaching the grates and immersing them in a concoction of warm water and dish soap. Post-soaking, scrub off any residual grime.

For gas grill users, routine inspection and cleaning of the burners are crucial. To commence, turn off the gas supply, remove the grates, and the barrier above the burners. Look out for trapped food particles or grease accumulation. Employ a stiff brush and a warm soapy water solution for a thorough cleaning.

In terms of interior cleaning, two or three times a season, or upon noticing significant grease build-up, the grill's interior requires attention. For charcoal grill users, this implies removing the coal grate and brushing out the ash. Gas grill users, on the other hand, should clean the barrier above the burners and the drip pan.

2. Storage Tips

Storage practices can dramatically impact your grill's lifespan. A quality grill cover is a sound investment, offering protection from weather elements and ensuring the grill remains dry, thus preventing rust formation. Ensure all your grilling utensils, cleaning brushes, and other accessories are stored together for easy access at grilling time.

During winter, particularly in colder climates, consider indoor storage options like a garage or shed if the grill will remain dormant. If indoor storage isn't feasible, a thorough cleaning followed by the use of a heavy-duty grill cover can effectively protect your grill.

3. Safety Checks

Safety checks are an integral part of grill maintenance, particularly for gas grills. Prior to the grilling season's onset, and sporadically throughout, ensure you check for gas leaks. Any leaks can be quickly found by applying the hose with a mild soap and water solution. By turning on the gas, the formation of bubbles indicates the presence of a leak.

Evaluate your grill's stability, ensuring it resides on a flat surface and exhibits no wobbling. A tipping grill, especially when hot, poses a significant danger. Also, conduct periodic inspections of your grill for signs of rust or damage, focusing on the burners, gas lines, and tank if you're using a gas grill.

Caring for your grill equipment may not be complicated or excessively time-consuming, but it demands regular attention. Consistent cleaning, appropriate storage, and routine safety checks will help maintain your grill in peak condition.

Grilling Techniques

Direct vs. Indirect Grilling: When to Use Each

Grilling is a culinary craft diverse in its techniques and methods. To achieve grilling perfection, understanding the nuances of the essential methods of direct and indirect grilling becomes pivotal. Mastery over these two styles and knowing when to employ them can significantly influence the gastronomic results of your grilling endeavors.

Direct Grilling

Direct grilling is arguably the quintessential grilling method, the one that usually resonates with our visual concept of grilling. As indicated by the name, this technique involves placing the food directly atop the heat source. Whether your grill operates on charcoal or gas, the core principle persists – the heat emanates directly from underneath, briskly searing the food's surface and sculpting a delectable char.

Ideally, direct grilling caters to smaller, thinner, and relatively tender pieces of meat and other fast-cooking foods. Picture grilling staples like hamburgers, hot dogs, steaks, chicken breasts, fish fillets, an array of vegetables, and skewers. When you choose to grill directly, the grill should be preheated, and the food necessitates a midway turn during the cooking process.

Indirect Grilling

In contrast, indirect grilling places the food close to the heat source rather than directly on top of it. For gas grills, this typically involves igniting one burner and positioning the food on the grill's unlit portion. On the other hand, if you're a charcoal grill enthusiast, this would mean accumulating the coals on one side of the grill and situating the food on the opposite side. In both scenarios, the grill is covered, eliciting a convection-like effect, akin to an oven.

Indirect grilling is a boon for grilling larger, tougher meat cuts that require extended cooking time, preventing them from burning or drying out. Think along the lines of whole chickens or turkeys, ribs, pork shoulders, and whole fish. It also serves as an excellent method for grilling foods marinated or basted with sweet or sugary sauces, which could otherwise quickly burn under direct heat.

The Combined Approach

There are instances, however, when a combination of both grilling techniques can lead to optimum results. Consider a large steak – initially searing it over direct heat aids in forming a flavorsome crust. Following this, the steak can be relocated to the indirect heat zone, allowing it to continue cooking without the risk of burning. Mastering these varied approaches will undeniably elevate your grilling exploits, bringing forth culinary delights that truly encapsulate the essence of grilling.

The Science of Smoking: Infusing Flavor into Your Food

Whether you're a seasoned pitmaster or just beginning to explore the world of barbecue, you've likely encountered the term "smoking." This practice extends beyond the realm of basic cooking; it transforms simple ingredients into flavor-packed, fragrant marvels. But what exactly unfolds during the smoking process?

Smoking can best be described as a harmonious symphony of flavors. This method champions slow, low-temperature cooking, typically between 180 and 220 degrees Fahrenheit, over the span of several hours. This prolonged, gentle approach achieves more than mere cooking; it infuses the food with an unparalleled smoky flavor and tenderizes it to a sublime, melt-in-your-mouth consistency.

Delving into the science behind the smoke, we find that when wood burns, it undergoes pyrolysis, breaking down into an array of gases, tars, and minuscule particles that collectively form smoke. As this smoke sways around the food, it bestows a unique flavor. However, its role extends further; it assists in preserving the food by forming a protective barrier that curtails bacterial growth.

The character of the smoke hinges on the type of wood utilized. Hardwoods such as hickory, oak, and maple yield a rich, potent flavor, whereas fruitwoods like apple, cherry, or peach generate a gentler, sweeter smoke. The choice of wood introduces a fresh avenue of creativity to your grilling endeavors.

The Maillard reaction, a chemical interplay between amino acids and reducing sugars, also plays an integral part in the smoking process. Occurring around 300 degrees Fahrenheit, this reaction catalyzes the delightful browning of the food's surface and the savory, complex flavors synonymous with grilled or roasted fare.

Given that smoking employs lower temperatures, the Maillard reaction doesn't occur as readily. Nonetheless, the smoke contributes to the browning of the food, albeit at a slower pace, resulting in a delectably smoky, mildly caramelized crust fondly termed as 'bark' within barbecue circles.

Moreover, smoking also regulates moisture. Slow cooking enables the internal fat and collagen within the meat to gradually break down, internally basting the meat and yielding a mouthwateringly tender texture. Concurrently, the smoke forms a 'pellicle' on the food's surface, locking in moisture and enhancing the flavor.

While the science of smoking offers a captivating perspective, the art of smoking is often what ensnares enthusiasts. Managing the fire, controlling the temperature, and ascertaining when the food has achieved the perfect smoke requires practice and patience. The outcome, however, is a feast steeped in rich, smoky flavor and cooked to tender perfection, proving every effort worthwhile.

Mastering Sear: The Secret to Texture and Flavor

The initial step in grilling often involves searing, a technique wherein your food - particularly meats - is subjected to high heat, creating a beautifully bronzed, flavor-packed crust. This method is pivotal in crafting an appealing texture, augmenting flavors, and preserving the succulent moisture within your grilled delights.

The Maillard reaction is the scientific explanation behind the magic of searing. It is a process wherein heat transforms the proteins and sugars present in food. The result is a cascade of hundreds of intricate chemical reactions, birthing robust flavors and intoxicating aromas that render grilled food irresistibly delicious. Louis-Camille Maillard, a French chemist, gave his name to this reaction.

Around the 300 degrees Fahrenheit mark, proteins and sugars on the food surface initiate their reaction, crafting a flavorful, brown crust. The trick lies in swiftly reaching this temperature - thus the high heat in searing - and maintaining it long enough for the Maillard reaction to occur, yet ensuring the food does not burn or dehydrate.

Mastering searing begins with high heat. Regardless of whether your grill is gas or charcoal-powered, aim to preheat it to approximately 500 degrees Fahrenheit for optimal searing results. A premium-quality grill with excellent heat retention capabilities can simplify this process.

Preparation of the food is the subsequent step. In the case of meats, ensure they are thoroughly patted dry prior to cooking; surplus moisture can disrupt the Maillard reaction. Seasoning the meat can further enhance the searing outcome, generating a delectable crust that traps the juices within.

When the moment to sear arrives, refrain from moving the food about. Permit the food to cook undisturbed to establish a smooth, even crust. Once the desired level of browning is achieved, the food is ready to be flipped.

A critical facet of searing lies in comprehending how to harmonize it with the overall cooking procedure. Searing is a rapid, high-heat process, yet it typically doesn't fully cook the food, particularly with thicker cuts of meat. Post-searing, the food often requires further cooking at reduced temperatures to attain the desired level of doneness without scorching the crust.

Rotisserie Grilling: The Hows and Whys

Rotisserie grilling, also known as spit-roasting, is a method of cooking where the food is skewered on a spit - a long, solid rod - and rotated over a heat source. Using this method, the food cooks evenly in its own juices, producing a dish that is tasty, moist, and nicely browned.

When food is cooked on a rotisserie, the rotation ensures an even distribution of heat. This not only allows for uniform cooking but also leads to a self-basting effect. As the food rotates, the fats and juices that would typically drip away are instead rolled back onto the food, enhancing its flavor and maintaining its moisture.

Getting started with rotisserie grilling involves some specific steps. Firstly, you'll need a grill equipped with a rotisserie burner and spit. You can also buy a rotisserie kit that fits your existing grill.

After setting up your rotisserie, it's time to prepare your food. This method works best with whole poultry or large, evenly shaped cuts of meat. You'll want to skewer your food onto the spit so that it's as balanced as possible. Remember, an unbalanced spit not only strains the motor but could also lead to uneven cooking.

Once skewered and balanced, the food is placed on the rotisserie at a medium heat. Avoid high temperatures as they can cause the outside of the food to burn before the inside is fully cooked. And once you have your food spinning, it's crucial to keep the grill lid firmly closed. This simple step helps maintain a steady temperature, facilitating even cooking. Using a meat thermometer will allow you to monitor the internal temperature accurately, ensuring your food is perfectly cooked.

Why, one may ask, should one opt for rotisserie grilling? There are several reasons why you might opt for rotisserie grilling. The most notable is that the self-basting nature of the process produces juicy, flavorful results that are difficult to achieve with other methods. The constant rotation also prevents hot spots and flare-ups, ensuring the food is cooked evenly without any burnt or undercooked areas.

Rubs, Sauces, Marinades, and More

Two of the most valuable tools for a griller's arsenal are marinades and rubs. Used correctly, they can take a cut of meat from standard to standout, infusing it with complex flavors and aiding in the cooking process.

Before cooking, you can soak foods, particularly meats, in a liquid solution: marinade. It fulfills dual roles of imparting flavor and tenderizing. When you immerse meats into the flavorful broth of the marinade, they absorb its ingredients and its essence, adding depth and character to the food. Simultaneously, the acidic components nestled within the marinade help break down tough proteins, making the meat more tender.

To concoct a successful marinade, you must judiciously blend three elemental ingredients: an acid, oil, and flavorings. The acidic element, be it vinegar, wine, or citrus juice, plays the key role of tenderizer, while the oil generously moisturizes the meat. Complementing these, the flavorings, which could range from herbs and spices to aromatic concoctions, infuse a flavorful punch.

The duration of marination varies with the meat type and size, spanning anywhere from a brief half an hour for seafood to a lengthy 24 hours for larger meat cuts.

Shifting our gaze to rubs, these are seasoning blends applied directly on the meat's surface. Unlike marinades, they do not possess the power of tenderization. Instead, their prowess lies in flavor enhancement and crafting a delightful crust or 'bark' upon the grilled meat.

There are two types of rubs: dry and wet. A dry rub is a harmonious blend of dried herbs and spices. In contrast, a wet rub evolves from its dry counterpart with the addition of moist ingredients like oil, mustard, or yogurt, yielding a paste.

To apply a rub, first pat your chosen meat dry. Then, sprinkle your rub over the meat, using your hands to ensure the seasonings adhere to the surface. After application, allow the meat a tranquil rest, granting the flavors time to permeate deeply. This could range from a swift 30 minutes to an entire night, depending on the depth of flavor you want.

So, which to use?

Whether to use a marinade or a rub depends on your desired outcome: if you want to tenderize a tougher cut of meat and infuse it with flavor, a marinade is your best bet. For giving a delicoius crust on the meat's surface, a rub is the way to go.

Expanding Your Grilling Horizons

Grilling for Events: From Family Gatherings to Tailgating

The charm of grilling transcends the realms of a simple home-cooked meal, extending its culinary allure to a variety of social events, be they intimate family gatherings or vivacious tailgating parties. Nothing quite captures the essence of communal bonding as the sizzling of food on a grill.

Let's consider the quintessential family gathering, be it a Sunday lunch or a festive occasion. Here, the grill plays the central role, around which memories are woven. The griller, donned in an apron, is the orchestral conductor, setting the rhythm for the gathering. Be it slow-cooked ribs that have everyone's mouthwatering or a more casual affair with burgers and hot dogs, the family grill offers a sense of familiarity and comfort.

Planning is the key to success when grilling for family events. You want to ensure that there is something for everyone. In addition to meat, consider offering a variety of vegetable options, grilled fruits, and even desserts like grilled peaches topped with ice cream. Create a timeline for your grilling to ensure that everything is cooked and served at the right time. With a bit of planning, you can transform a simple family gathering into a gourmet affair.

In stark contrast, tailgating is the social currency of sporting events, a pre-game ritual that serves as the perfect icebreaker among fans. It's an event where the grill is no longer a kitchen appliance but transforms into a symbol of shared passion. Here, the stakes are different - the foods are portable, often handheld, devoured with a voracious appetite amped up by sporting enthusiasm. Think bratwursts, skewers, and sliders, food that's easy to handle and hearty enough to keep the energy high for the big game.

When tailgating, your grill's portability becomes a significant factor. Portable grills that can fit in the trunk of a car are ideal. You should also take into consideration the grill's ability to maintain heat over a few hours, as tailgating can be an all-day event. Also, remember that at a tailgating event, the food should be easy to eat standing up and should be ready quickly.

Whether it's a family gathering or tailgating, remember that grilling for an event isn't just about the food; it's about the experience. For family gatherings, the grill serves as a backdrop for creating memories, and for tailgating, it's a symbol of team spirit and shared enthusiasm.

Grilling is a social event in and of itself. Each sizzle and flip of the food is a testament to this age-old tradition that brings us together in celebration, be it familial or communal. So the next time you fire up that grill, remember, you're not just cooking a meal; you're crafting an experience, an event that will be remembered long after the last morsel has been devoured.

The World on Your Grill: International Grilling Techniques

The symphony of sizzles and crackles from a well-tended grill is a melody that transcends geographical boundaries. Every corner of the globe bears a unique grilling tradition, infusing rich flavors, and techniques into a universal passion for flame-cooked fare. Embrace the world on your grill by exploring these diverse grilling traditions, each with a story to tell.

In the sultry corners of South America, you'll find the Argentine 'asado'. The heartbeat of every social gathering, 'asado' is more than a barbecue. It is an art, a ritual of slowly grilling meats, often whole, on a parrilla or iron grill. The wood-fired grills lend an intense smoky flavor to the meats, and the secret to their juicy, tender texture lies in the slow, patient cooking technique. Chimichurri, a vibrant blend of parsley, garlic, vinegar, and oil, serves as the quintessential accompaniment, adding a burst of freshness to balance the rich meats.

Traveling halfway across the globe, you land in Japan, home to 'Yakitori' - skewered chicken grilled over a charcoal fire. Each skewer, meticulously threaded with bite-sized pieces of chicken, is grilled to perfection and served with 'tare', a sweet and savory glaze, or simply seasoned with salt. The hallmark of 'Yakitori' lies in its simplicity and reverence for the ingredient, transforming chicken into an exquisite, flavorful delight.

Set foot in the Mediterranean, and you encounter 'Souvlaki' from Greece. Juicy morsels of marinated pork are skewered and grilled to a tantalizing crispness, then served wrapped in warm pita bread with tzatziki sauce, a cooling cucumber and yogurt condiment. Here, the grill not only transforms the meat but brings a warming, toasted flavor to the pita, adding depth to the whole ensemble.

Venturing into the Middle East, 'Kebabs' reign supreme. Whether it's the Persian 'Koobideh', minced meat kebabs seasoned with a medley of spices and grilled on wide, flat skewers, or the Turkish 'Shish Kebab', chunks of marinated meat and vegetables threaded onto a skewer, kebabs symbolize the Middle Eastern grilling tradition. Paired with flatbreads, salads, and dips, they offer a feast for the senses.

Exploring the world on your grill brings a dash of adventure to your backyard. It allows you to travel gastronomically, appreciating the nuances and traditions that make each grilling culture unique. This culinary journey not only introduces you to a multitude of flavors and techniques but also allows you to infuse your grilling repertoire with a global flair. Let your grill be your passport, as you journey through the sizzling, aromatic lanes of global grilling traditions.

In the following chapter, you will find a section also dedicated to traditional recipes from various parts of the world.

Recipes

Red Meat

1. Smoky BBQ Beef Brisket

Preparation time: 10 minutes   **Cooking time:** 7-9 hours
Servings: 8

Ingredients:
- 5 lbs beef brisket
- 2 tbsp brown sugar
- 2 tbsp smoked paprika
- 1 tbsp black pepper
- 1 tbsp sea salt
- 1 tbsp chili powder
- 2 tsp garlic powder
- 2 tsp onion powder
- 1 tsp cayenne pepper
- 1/2 cup BBQ sauce

Directions:
In a bowl, combine the brown sugar, smoked paprika, black pepper, sea salt, chili powder, garlic powder, onion powder, and cayenne pepper to create your rub. Apply the rub all over the brisket, covering all sides.

Preheat your grill to 250°F (120°C). Place the brisket fat side up on the grill and cook for 5 to 6 hours, or until the internal temperature reaches 165 degrees Fahrenheit (74°C).

Remove the brisket from the grill and wrap it in aluminum foil. Putting it back on the grill, let it cook until the internal temperature reaches 195°F (90°C). This should take another 2-3 hours.

Let the brisket rest for about 20-30 minutes before slicing against the grain. Serve with BBQ sauce.

Preparation Tips: Slow and low is the key to a tender brisket. Don't rush the cooking process.

Nutritional Value per Serving: Calories 411.3, Fat 18.2g, Carbohydrates 12.3g, Protein 50.8g

---

2. Savory Rib-Eye Steak with Herb Butter

Preparation time: 10 minutes   **Cooking time:** 5 minutes
Servings: 4

Ingredients:
- 4 rib-eye steaks (about 1.5 inches thick)
- 2 tbsp olive oil
- Salt and black pepper to taste

For the Herb Butter:
- 1/2 cup unsalted butter, softened
- 2 tbsp fresh chopped parsley
- 1 tbsp fresh chopped chives
- 1 clove garlic, minced
- Salt and black pepper to taste

Directions:
Preheat your grill to high heat. Season the steaks on both sides with salt, olive oil, and black pepper.

For medium-rare, grill the steaks on each side for about 4 to 5 minutes, or continue grilling until desired doneness.

While the steaks are grilling, prepare the herb butter by combining the softened butter, parsley, chives, garlic, salt, and pepper in a bowl. Mix until well combined.

Once the steaks are done, immediately top them with a dollop of herb butter and let them rest for a few minutes before serving.

Shopping Tips: Choose steaks that are evenly cut to ensure consistent cooking. For the herb butter, fresh herbs are preferable for maximum flavor.

Preparation Tips: Let the steaks come to room temperature before grilling for even cooking. Also, let the steaks rest after grilling to allow the juices to redistribute.

Nutritional Value per Serving: Calories 649, Fat 51.3g, Carbohydrates 1g, Protein 49.8g

---

3. BBQ Beef Ribs with Honey Glaze

Preparation time: 10 minutes

Cooking time: 3 hours

Servings: 6

Ingredients:
- 4 lbs beef ribs
- Salt and black pepper to taste

For the Honey Glaze:
- 1/2 cup honey
- 1/4 cup apple cider vinegar
- 1/4 cup Dijon mustard
- 2 cloves garlic, minced
- 1 tsp chili powder
- 1/2 tsp salt

Directions:
Preheat your grill to 275°F (135°C). Add salt and black pepper to the ribs.
Grill the ribs, bone side down, for about 2.5-3 hours, or until the meat is tender. While the ribs are grilling, prepare the honey glaze by combining the honey, apple cider vinegar, Dijon mustard, garlic, chili powder, and salt in a saucepan. Simmer over medium heat for about 10 minutes, or until the glaze thickens.
Brush the ribs with the honey glaze during the last 30 minutes of grilling. Before serving, let the ribs rest for a few minutes.

Shopping Tips: Look for ribs with a good amount of meat on them, not just bone.

Preparation Tips: Apply the glaze during the last part of cooking to prevent it from burning.

Nutritional Value per Serving: Calories 752, Fat 40.3g, Carbohydrates 44.5g, Protein 56.5g

4. <u>Grilled Skirt Steak with Chimichurri Sauce</u>

Preparation time: 10 minutes   **Cooking time:** 6-8 minutes
Servings: 4

Ingredients:
- *2 lbs skirt steak*
- *2 tbsp olive oil*
- *Salt and black pepper to taste*

For the Chimichurri Sauce:
- *1 cup fresh parsley*
- *1/2 cup olive oil*
- *1/3 cup red wine vinegar*
- *2 cloves garlic*
- *1/2 tsp crushed red pepper flakes*
- *Salt and black pepper to taste*

Directions:
Preheat your grill to high heat. Season the steak with salt, olive oil, and black pepper. For medium-rare, grill the steaks on each side for about 3 to 4 minutes, or continue grilling until desired doneness.

While the steak is grilling, prepare the chimichurri sauce by combining the parsley, olive oil, red wine vinegar, garlic, red pepper flakes, salt, and black pepper in a blender. Blend until smooth.

Once the steak is done, before slicing, let it rest for a few minutes. Put the chimichurri sauce on top and serve.

Shopping Tips: Skirt steak is a flavorful cut that grills up quickly, look for even thickness to ensure even cooking.

Preparation Tips: Slice the skirt steak against the grain for maximum tenderness.

Nutritional Value per Serving: Calories 653, Fat 44.5g, Carbohydrates 2.1g, Protein 52.1g

5. Grilled T-Bone Steaks with BBQ Rub

Preparation time: 10 minutes   **Cooking time:** 8-10 minutes
Servings: 4

Ingredients:
- *4 T-Bone steaks (about 1 inch thick)*
- *Olive oil for brushing*

For the BBQ Rub:
- *2 tbsp brown sugar*
- *1 tbsp smoked paprika*
- *1 tsp garlic powder*
- *1 tsp onion powder*
- *1/2 tsp black pepper*
- *1/2 tsp salt*

Directions:
Preheat your grill to high heat. On both sides, brush the steaks with olive oil. Prepare the BBQ rub by combining the smoked paprika, brown sugar, onion powder, garlic powder, black pepper, and salt in a bowl. Rub this mixture all over the steaks. For medium-rare, grill the steaks for about 4-5 minutes on each side or until desired doneness. Let them rest for a few minutes before serving.

Preparation Tips: Let the steaks rest after grilling to allow the juices to redistribute.

Nutritional Value per Serving: Calories 648.6, Fat 42.5g, Carbohydrates 4.5g, Protein 57.9g

---

6. Grilled T-Bone Steaks with Garlic Herb Butter

Preparation Time: 10 minutes   **Cooking Time:** 10 minutes
Servings: 4

Ingredients:
- *4 T-bone steaks*
- *Salt and pepper to taste*
- *1/2 cup unsalted butter, softened*
- *2 cloves garlic, minced*
- *1 tbsp fresh chopped parsley*
- *1 tbsp fresh chopped chives*

Directions:
Preheat your grill to high heat.
Season the T-bone steaks with salt and pepper on both sides.
For medium-rare, grill the steaks for about 4-5 minutes on each side or until desired doneness.
While the steaks are grilling, combine the softened butter, minced garlic, parsley, and chives in a bowl. Stir until well combined.

Once the steaks are done, top each one with a dollop of the garlic herb butter. Let the steaks rest for a few minutes before serving.

Shopping Tips: When buying T-bone steaks, look for ones with a clear, defined bone and plenty of marbling.

Preparation Tips: Let the steaks sit at room temperature for 30 minutes before grilling for even cooking.

Nutritional Value per Serving: Calories 620.2, Fat 47.6g, Carbohydrates 1g, Protein 445g

7. <u>Grilled Beef Kebabs with Vegetables</u>

Preparation Time: 15 minutes   **Cooking Time:** 10 minutes
Servings: 8

Ingredients:
- 2 lbs beef sirloin, cut into 1-inch cubes
- 2 bell peppers, cut into 1-inch pieces
- 2 zucchinis, cut into 1-inch rounds
- 1 red onion, cut into 1-inch pieces
- 1/4 cup olive oil
- Salt and pepper to taste

Directions:
Preheat your grill to medium-high heat.
Thread the beef, bell peppers, zucchinis, and red onion onto skewers, alternating as you go.
Brush the kebabs with olive oil and season with salt and pepper.
Grill the kebabs for about 4-5 minutes on each side, or until the beef is cooked to your desired level of doneness.
Let the kebabs rest for a few minutes before serving.

Shopping Tips: You can substitute beef sirloin with other cuts like ribeye or tenderloin.

Preparation Tips:
Wooden skewers should be soaked in water for 30 minutes before grilling to prevent them from burning.

Nutritional Value per Serving: Calories 342, Fat 21.4g, Carbohydrates 4.7g, Protein 33.5g

8. Classic BBQ Beef Ribs

Preparation Time: 15 minutes   **Cooking Time:** 2.5 hours
Servings: 4

Ingredients:
- 4 lbs beef ribs
- 1 cup BBQ sauce
- 1/4 cup brown sugar
- 2 tbsp paprika
- Salt and pepper to taste

Directions: Preheat your grill to 225°F (low heat).
In a bowl, mix together the brown sugar, paprika, salt, and pepper.
Rub the spice mixture onto the beef ribs, coating them thoroughly.
Place the ribs bone-side down on the grill. Close the lid and let them cook for about 2 hours.
Brush the ribs with BBQ sauce and continue to cook for another 30 minutes.
Before serving, let the ribs rest for a few minutes.

Nutritional Value per Serving: Calories 804.9, Fat 52.1g, Carbohydrates 24.5g, Protein 63.3g

9. BBQ Beef Brisket

Preparation Time: 20 minutes   **Cooking Time:** 6 hours
Servings: 8

Ingredients:
- 5 lbs beef brisket
- 1 cup BBQ sauce
- 1/4 cup brown sugar
- 2 tbsp smoked paprika
- Salt and pepper to taste

Directions: Preheat your grill to 250°F (low heat).
In a bowl, mix together the smoked paprika, salt, brown sugar, and pepper.
Rub the spice mixture onto the beef brisket, coating it thoroughly.
Place the brisket fat-side up on the grill. Close the lid and let it cook for about 5 hours.
Brush the brisket with BBQ sauce and continue to cook for another hour.
Let the brisket rest for a few minutes before slicing and serving.

Shopping Tips: Look for a beef brisket with a thick layer of fat on top. As a result, the meat will keep moist as it cooks.

Nutritional Value per Serving: Calories 658, Fat 31.2g, Carbohydrates 22.03g, Protein 74.7g

10. **Smoky BBQ Beef Skewers**

Preparation Time: 20 minutes (plus 1 hour for marinating)
Cooking Time: 10-12 minutes
Servings: 4

Ingredients:
- 2 lbs beef sirloin, cut into cubes
- 1 cup BBQ sauce
- 1 tbsp smoked paprika
- Salt and pepper to taste

Directions: In a bowl, combine the BBQ sauce, smoked paprika, salt, and pepper. Add the beef cubes and toss to coat. Cover and refrigerate for at least 1 hour.
Preheat your grill to medium heat.
Thread the beef cubes onto skewers.
The skewers should be grilled for 5 to 6 minutes on each side, until the beef is cooked to your liking.

Nutritional Value per Serving: Calories 449.8, Fat 14.5g, Carbohydrates 31.02g, Protein 52.2g

---

11. **BBQ Beef Sliders**

Preparation Time: 15 minutes
Servings: 8

Cooking Time: 10 minutes

Ingredients:
- 1 lb ground beef
- 1/2 cup BBQ sauce
- 1/2 cup finely chopped onion
- Salt and pepper to taste
- 8 slider buns

Directions: In a bowl, combine the ground beef, half of the BBQ sauce, onion, salt, and pepper. Mix until well combined.
Form the mixture into 8 small patties.
Preheat your grill to medium heat.
Grill the patties for 3-4 minutes on each side, until cooked through. During the last minute of cooking, brush the patties with the remaining BBQ sauce.
Serve the patties on slider buns.

Nutritional Value per Serving: Calories 254.5, Fat 11.2g, Carbohydrates 24.5g, Protein 13.5g

12. BBQ Beef Brisket Sandwiches

Preparation Time: 20 minutes **Cooking Time:** 3-4 hours
Servings: 8

Ingredients:
- 2 lbs beef brisket
- 2 cups BBQ sauce
- 1 large onion, sliced
- 2 cloves garlic, minced
- Salt and pepper to taste
- 8 hamburger buns

Directions: Season the brisket with salt and pepper.
Preheat the grill to low heat and set it up for indirect grilling.
Place the brisket on the grill, cover, and cook for 3-4 hours, until it is tender. Check and turn occasionally, basting with BBQ sauce in the last hour of cooking.
Remove the brisket from the grill and let it rest for 10 minutes before slicing thinly.
Serve the sliced brisket on hamburger buns, topped with additional BBQ sauce if desired.

Shopping Tips: Choose a beef brisket with plenty of marbling, as this will result in a juicier end product.

Nutritional Value per Serving: Calories 474.7, Fat 16.7g, Carbohydrates 44.5g, Protein 33.4g

13. BBQ Beef Ribs

Preparation Time: 15 minutes **Cooking Time:** 3-4 hours
Servings: 4

Ingredients:
- 2 racks of beef ribs
- 1 cup BBQ sauce
- Salt and pepper to taste

Directions: Season the ribs with salt and pepper.
Preheat your grill to low heat and set it up for indirect grilling.
Cook the ribs on the grill with the lid closed for 3-4 hours, until they are tender. Check and turn occasionally, basting with BBQ sauce in the last hour of cooking.
Serve the ribs with additional BBQ sauce if desired.

Shopping Tips: When buying beef ribs, look for racks with a good amount of meat on them and not too much fat.

Nutritional Value per Serving: Calories 773.2, Fat 43.7g, Carbohydrates 36.2g, Protein 58.9g

---

14.   Spicy BBQ Beef Kebabs

Preparation Time: 15 minutes + marination time   **Cooking Time:** 15 minutes
Servings: 4

Ingredients:
- *2 lbs beef sirloin, cut into 1-inch cubes*
- *1 cup spicy BBQ sauce*
- *1 bell pepper, cut into 1-inch pieces*
- *1 onion, cut into 1-inch pieces*
- *8 skewers*

Directions: Place the beef cubes in a large bowl, add the BBQ sauce, stir to coat, cover, and marinate in the refrigerator for at least 2 hours, or overnight if possible. Preheat your grill to medium-high heat.
On the skewers, alternate threading bell pepper and onion pieces with beef cubes. Grill the kebabs for about 15 minutes, turning occasionally, until the beef is cooked to your desired level of doneness.

Shopping Tips: When shopping for beef sirloin, look for a cut with a good balance of meat and fat for the most flavorful kebabs.

Nutritional Value per Serving: Calories 473.7, Fat 24.6g, Carbohydrates 21.3g, Protein 46.1g

---

15.   BBQ Beef Tacos

Preparation Time: 20 minutes   **Cooking Time:** 10 minutes
Servings: 8

Ingredients:
- *2 lbs beef flank steak*
- *1 cup BBQ sauce*
- *Salt and pepper to taste*
- *8 soft taco shells*
- *Toppings: shredded lettuce, diced tomatoes, shredded*
- *cheese, salsa, sour cream*

Directions: Season the flank steak with salt and pepper, then coat it with the BBQ sauce.

Preheat your grill to high heat.

Grill the steak for about 5 minutes on each side, or until it has reached your desired level of doneness.

Remove the steak from the grill and let it rest for a few minutes. Then slice it thinly against the grain.

Serve the sliced steak in the soft taco shells, topped with your choice of toppings.

Shopping Tips: When shopping for flank steak, look for a piece that is even in thickness to ensure that it cooks evenly.

Nutritional Value per Serving (excluding toppings): Calories 351.3, Fat 15.5g, Carbohydrates 24.7g, Protein 31.4g

---

16.   BBQ Beef Ribs with a Coffee Rub

Preparation Time: 15 minutes   **Cooking Time:** 4 hours
Servings: 4

Ingredients:
- 4 lbs beef ribs
- 1/4 cup ground coffee
- 1/4 cup brown sugar
- 1 tablespoon smoked paprika
- 1 teaspoon chili powder
- 1 teaspoon salt
- 1/2 teaspoon black pepper
- BBQ sauce for serving (optional)

Directions: Mix the ground coffee, brown sugar, smoked paprika, chili powder, salt, and pepper together in a bowl.

Rub the mixture all over the beef ribs, then let them sit for at least 15 minutes to absorb the flavors.

Preheat your grill to low heat.

Cook the ribs on the grill for about 4 hours, or until they are tender and the meat pulls easily from the bone. Serve with BBQ sauce on the side, if desired.

Shopping Tips: When shopping for beef ribs, look for ribs with a good amount of meat on them and not too much fat.

Nutritional Value per Serving: Calories 902, Fat 66.5g, Carbohydrates 11.3g, Protein 71.4g

17.   Grilled Beef Sliders with BBQ Sauce

Preparation Time: 15 minutes   **Cooking Time:** 15 minutes
Servings: 16

Ingredients:
- 2 lbs ground beef
- Salt and pepper to taste
- 1 cup BBQ sauce
- 16 slider buns
- Toppings: lettuce, tomato, pickles, onions

Directions: Shape the ground beef into 16 small patties, then season them with salt and pepper.
Preheat your grill to medium-high heat.
Grill the patties for about 3-4 minutes on each side.
During the last minute of cooking, brush the patties with BBQ sauce.
Serve the patties on the slider buns, topped with your choice of toppings.

Shopping Tips: When shopping for ground beef, choose beef with a higher fat content (around 15-20%) for juicier sliders.

Nutritional Value per Serving (excluding toppings): Calories 251.4, Fat 11.2g, Carbohydrates 20.6g, Protein 15.5g

18.   Grilled Lamb Chops with Rosemary and Garlic

Preparation Time: 10 minutes   **Cooking Time:** 15 minutes
Servings: 4

Ingredients:
- 8 lamb chops
- 1/4 cup olive oil
- 2 tablespoons fresh rosemary, finely chopped
- 4 garlic cloves, minced
- Salt and pepper to taste

Directions: In a bowl, mix the olive oil, rosemary, garlic, salt, and pepper. Coat the lamb chops with this mixture and let them marinate for at least an hour.
Preheat your grill to medium heat.
Grill the lamb chops for about 7 minutes on each side.

Nutritional Value per Serving: Calories 397, Fat 28.9g, Carbohydrates 2.2g, Protein 31.2g

19. Greek-Style Grilled Lamb Kebabs

Preparation Time: 10 minutes   **Cooking Time:** 10 minutes
Servings: 4

Ingredients:
- *1 lb lamb, cut into 1-inch cubes*
- *Juice of 1 lemon*
- *1/4 cup olive oil*
- *1 tablespoon dried oregano*
- *1 tablespoon fresh thyme, chopped*
- *Salt and pepper to taste*
- *Wooden or metal skewers*

Directions: In a bowl, combine the lemon juice, olive oil, oregano, thyme, salt, and pepper. Add the lamb and let it marinate for at least an hour.
Preheat your grill to medium-high heat.
Thread the lamb onto the skewers, then grill for about 10 minutes, turning occasionally, until they're cooked to your liking.

Shopping Tips: You can use any cut of lamb for this recipe, but leg of lamb or shoulder works particularly well.

Nutritional Value per Serving: Calories 356, Fat 24.5g, Carbohydrates 2.3g, Protein 25.2g

---

20. Lamb Burger with Mint and Feta

Preparation Time: 15 minutes   **Cooking Time:** 10 minutes
Servings: 4

Ingredients:
- *1 lb ground lamb*
- *1/2 cup crumbled feta cheese*
- *1/4 cup fresh mint leaves, finely chopped*
- *2 tablespoons olive oil*
- *1/2 cup Greek yogurt*
- *Salt and pepper to taste*
- *4 hamburger buns*

Directions: In a bowl, mix the ground lamb, half of the feta cheese, half of the mint, salt, and pepper. Form into 4 patties.
In another bowl, mix the Greek yogurt, remaining mint, and a pinch of salt. Set aside.
Preheat your grill to medium-high heat. Brush the lamb patties with olive oil and grill for about 5 minutes on each side.
Toast the hamburger buns on the grill, then assemble the burgers with the lamb patties, remaining feta, and the mint-yogurt sauce.

Shopping Tips: Fresh mint is essential for this recipe. Dried mint will not give the same flavor.

Nutritional Value per Serving: Calories 453, Fat 30.4g, Carbohydrates 18.9g, Protein 24.8g

---

21.   Barbecued Lamb Ribs with Honey and Rosemary

Preparation Time: 10 minutes   **Cooking Time:** 2 hours
Servings: 4

Ingredients:
- *1 rack of lamb ribs*
- *1/4 cup honey*
- *1/4 cup apple cider vinegar*
- *2 tablespoons fresh rosemary, finely chopped*
- *Salt and pepper to taste*

Directions: Preheat your grill to low heat.
In a bowl, mix the honey, vinegar, rosemary, salt, and pepper. Brush this mixture onto the lamb ribs.
Grill the ribs over indirect heat for about 2 hours, or until they're tender and the meat pulls away from the bone easily. Brush with more glaze every 30 minutes.

Nutritional Value per Serving: Calories 398, Fat 26.2g, Carbohydrates 20.1g, Protein 26.3g

---

22.   Grilled Lamb Leg with Lemon and Oregano

Preparation Time: 15 minutes   **Cooking Time:** 1 hour
Servings: 6

Ingredients:
- *1 boneless leg of lamb (about 2 lbs)*
- *Juice of 2 lemons*
- *1/4 cup olive oil*
- *1 tablespoon dried oregano*
- *4 garlic cloves, minced*
- *Salt and pepper to taste*

Directions: In a bowl, mix the lemon juice, olive oil, oregano, garlic, salt, and pepper. Rub this mixture all over the lamb leg and let it marinate for at least 4 hours, or overnight.

Preheat your grill to medium-low heat. Cook the lamb leg over indirect heat for about 1 hour. Let it rest for 10 minutes before slicing.

Shopping Tips: A boneless leg of lamb is easier to slice and serve, but you can also use a bone-in leg for this recipe.

Nutritional Value per Serving: Calories 304, Fat 16.5g, Carbohydrates 2.3g, Protein 34.5g

Poultry

23.   Honey BBQ Chicken Wings

Preparation Time: 10 minutes   **Cooking Time:** 30 minutes
Servings: 4

Ingredients:
- 2 lbs chicken wings
- Salt and pepper to taste
- 1 cup BBQ sauce
- 1/4 cup honey
- 1 teaspoon smoked paprika
- Green onions for garnish

Directions: Preheat your grill to medium-high heat.
Season the chicken wings with salt and pepper.
Grill the wings for about 15 minutes on each side.
In a large bowl, combine the BBQ sauce, honey, and smoked paprika.
Toss the grilled wings in the sauce, then top with shredded green onions before serving.

Shopping Tips: When shopping for chicken wings, you can buy whole wings and separate them yourself, or look for pre-cut wingettes and drumettes for convenience.

Nutritional Value per Serving: Calories 448.9, Fat 23.4g, Carbohydrates 36.6g, Protein 26.5g

---

24.   BBQ Chicken Pizza

Preparation Time: 20 minutes   **Cooking Time:** 15 minutes
Servings: 4

Ingredients:
- 1 pizza dough
- 1/2 cup BBQ sauce
- 1 cup shredded mozzarella cheese
- 1 chicken breast, grilled and sliced
- 1/2 red onion, thinly sliced
- Cilantro for garnish

Directions: Preheat your grill to medium-high heat.
Roll out the pizza dough on a lightly floured surface to your desired thickness.
Grill one side of the dough for about 2-3 minutes, or until it begins to puff up.
Flip the dough over, then quickly spread the BBQ sauce on top, followed by the cheese, grilled chicken slices, and red onions.
Close the grill lid and cook for another 5-7 minutes, or until the cheese is melted and the dough is crispy.
Garnish with fresh cilantro before serving.

Shopping Tips: When shopping for pizza dough, you can often find fresh dough in the bakery section of your grocery store, or you can use a premade pizza crust for convenience.

Nutritional Value per Serving: Calories 447.9, Fat 12.4g, Carbohydrates 52.1g, Protein 28.9g

---

25.   Grilled Chicken Caesar Salad

Preparation Time: 15 minutes   **Cooking Time:** 20 minutes
Servings: 4

Ingredients:
- 2 chicken breasts
- Salt and pepper to taste
- 1 head romaine lettuce, chopped
- 1 cup croutons
- 1/2 cup grated Parmesan cheese
- Caesar dressing to taste

Directions: Preheat your grill to medium-high heat.
Season the chicken breasts with salt and pepper, then grill for about 10 minutes on each side, or until fully cooked.
Let the chicken rest for a few minutes, then slice it into thin strips.
In a large bowl, combine the chopped lettuce, croutons, and Parmesan cheese. Add the grilled chicken and Caesar dressing, then toss to combine.

Shopping Tips: Romaine lettuce is the traditional choice for Caesar salad, but you could also use mixed greens or spinach for a different twist.

Nutritional Value per Serving: Calories 340.3, Fat 16.8g, Carbohydrates 15.6g, Protein 33.7g

---

26.   BBQ Chicken Kabobs

Preparation Time: 15 minutes   **Cooking Time:** 15 minutes
Servings: 4

Ingredients:
- 2 chicken breasts, cut into cubes
- 1/2 cup BBQ sauce
- 1 red bell pepper, cut into chunks
- 1 green bell pepper, cut into chunks
- 1 red onion, cut into chunks
- Skewers

Directions: Preheat your grill to medium-high heat.
Toss the chicken cubes in the BBQ sauce, then thread them onto the skewers, alternating with chunks of bell pepper and red onion.
Grill the kabobs for about 7 minutes on each side, or until the chicken is fully cooked.

Nutritional Value per Serving: Calories 272.1, Fat 5.6g, Carbohydrates 23.6g, Protein 32.1g

27.   Grilled Chicken Quesadillas

Preparation Time: 15 minutes

Cooking Time: 10 minutes

Servings: 4

Ingredients:
- 2 chicken breasts, grilled and shredded
- 1 cup shredded cheddar cheese
- 4 flour tortillas
- 1/2 cup salsa
- Sour cream and guacamole for serving

Directions: Preheat your grill to medium heat.

Sprinkle cheese and shredded chicken over half of each tortilla, then fold over to close.

Grill the quesadillas for about 3-4 minutes on each side, or until the tortillas are crispy and the cheese is melted.

Serve with sour cream, salsa, and guacamole on the side.

Shopping Tips: For a more flavorful quesadilla, you could add some grilled onions or bell peppers to the filling.

Nutritional Value per Serving: Calories 411, Fat 21.3g, Carbohydrates 28.9g, Protein 29.9g

28.   Grilled Chicken Alfredo Pizza

Preparation Time: 20 minutes

Cooking Time: 15 minutes

Servings: 4

Ingredients:
- 1 pizza dough
- 1/2 cup Alfredo sauce
- 1 chicken breast, grilled and sliced
- 1 cup shredded mozzarella cheese
- 1/2 cup sliced mushrooms
- 1/2 cup sliced bell peppers
- 1/2 cup sliced red onions

Directions: Preheat your grill to medium-high heat.

Roll out the pizza dough and grill it for about 2-3 minutes on one side.

Flip the dough over. On the grilled side, spread the Alfredo sauce.

Top with sliced chicken, shredded cheese, and vegetables.

Grill for another 10-12 minutes, or until the cheese is bubbly.

Shopping Tips: For added flavor, you can marinate the chicken in some Italian seasoning before grilling.

Nutritional Value per Serving: Calories 522, Fat 21.3g, Carbohydrates 48.6g, Protein 34.5g

29.   Grilled Chicken Tacos with Mango Salsa

Preparation Time: 20 minutes   **Cooking Time:** 15 minutes
Servings: 4

Ingredients:
- *2 chicken breasts*
- *1 packet taco seasoning*
- *8 small tortillas*
- *1 cup chopped mango*
- *1/2 cup chopped red onion*
- *1/2 cup chopped cilantro*
- *Juice of 1 lime*
- *Salt to taste*

Directions: Preheat your grill to medium-high heat.

Season the chicken breasts with taco seasoning, then grill for about 10 minutes on each side, or until fully cooked.

Prepare the salsa while the chicken is grilling. So, combine chopped mango, red onion, cilantro, lime juice, and salt.

Slice the grilled chicken and serve it in the tortillas, topped with mango salsa.

Shopping Tips: Look for ripe, but firm mangos for the best salsa.

Nutritional Value per Serving: Calories 378, Fat 9.7g, Carbohydrates 41.4g, Protein 33.8g

---

30.   Grilled Chicken Skewers with Peanut Sauce

Preparation Time: 15 minutes   **Cooking Time:** 15 minutes
Servings: 4

Ingredients:
- *2 chicken breasts, cut into cubes*
- *Salt and pepper to taste*
- *Skewers*
- *1/2 cup peanut butter*
- *1/4 cup soy sauce*
- *2 tablespoons honey*
- *1 tablespoon lime juice*
- *1 teaspoon minced garlic*
- *1/2 teaspoon chili flakes*

Directions: Preheat your grill to medium-high heat.

Season the chicken cubes with salt and pepper, then thread them onto the skewers.

Grill the skewers for about 7 minutes on each side, or until the chicken is fully cooked.

Prepare the peanut sauce while the chicken is grilling, by combining peanut butter, soy sauce, honey, lime juice, minced garlic, and chili flakes.

Nutritional Value per Serving: Calories 451, Fat 18.9g, Carbohydrates 18.9g, Protein 37.6g

31. Grilled Chicken Parmesan

Preparation Time: 10 minutes   **Cooking Time:** 15 minutes
Servings: 4

Ingredients:
- 2 chicken breasts
- Salt and pepper to taste
- 1 cup marinara sauce
- 1 cup shredded mozzarella cheese
- 1/2 cup grated Parmesan cheese
- 1/4 cup chopped fresh basil

Directions: Preheat your grill to medium-high heat.
Season the chicken breasts with salt and pepper, then grill for about 6-7 minutes on each side. Top each chicken breast with marinara sauce, shredded mozzarella, and Parmesan cheese.
Close the grill lid and cook for another 2-3 minutes, or until the cheese is melted and bubbly. Sprinkle with fresh basil before serving.

Shopping Tips: For the best flavor, use fresh mozzarella and high-quality marinara sauce.

Nutritional Value per Serving: Calories 372, Fat 16.3g, Carbs 8.1g, Protein 47.3g

---

32. Honey Mustard Grilled Chicken Salad

Preparation Time: 15 minutes   **Cooking Time:** 15 minutes
Servings: 4

Ingredients:
- 2 chicken breasts
- Salt and pepper to taste
- 6 cups mixed salad greens
- 1 cup cherry tomatoes, halved
- 1 cucumber, sliced
- 1/2 red onion, thinly sliced
- 1/2 cup honey mustard dressing

Directions: Preheat your grill to medium-high heat.
Season the chicken breasts with salt and pepper, then grill for about 6-7 minutes on each side.
Slice the grilled chicken and add it to a large salad bowl along with the cherry tomatoes, salad greens, red onion, and cucumber. Season with honey mustard dressing and stir.

Nutritional Value per Serving: Calories 379, Fat 15.4g, Carbohydrates 20.4g, Protein 34.5g

33. Herb Grilled Turkey Breast

Preparation Time: 10 minutes   **Cooking Time:** 45 minutes
Servings: 6

Ingredients:
- *1 boneless turkey breast (about 2 lbs)*
- *2 tablespoons olive oil*
- *2 teaspoons dried rosemary*
- *2 teaspoons dried thyme*
- *Salt and pepper to taste*

Directions: Preheat your grill to medium heat.
Brush the turkey breast with olive oil, then season with salt, thyme, rosemary, and pepper.
Grill the turkey breast for about 45 minutes, turning occasionally, until it reaches an internal temperature of 165 degrees F.
Let the turkey rest for a few minutes before slicing and serving.

Shopping Tips: Look for a boneless turkey breast that's not pre-seasoned, so you can control the flavorings yourself.

Nutritional Value per Serving: Calories 218, Fat 5.2g, Carbs 0.9g, Protein 44.6g

---

34. Grilled Turkey Burgers with Avocado

Preparation Time: 15 minutes   **Cooking Time:** 15 minutes
Servings: 4

Ingredients:
- *1 lb ground turkey*
- *1/2 onion, finely chopped*
- *1/2 cup breadcrumbs*
- *1 egg*
- *Salt and pepper to taste*
- *4 hamburger buns*
- *1 avocado, sliced*

Directions: Preheat your grill to medium-high heat.
In a bowl, combine the ground turkey, onion, breadcrumbs, salt, egg, and pepper. Form into 4 patties.
Grill the patties for about 7 minutes on each side, or until fully cooked.
Serve the burgers on buns with sliced avocado and your choice of other toppings.

Shopping Tips: Choose ground turkey that's at least 93% lean for a healthier option.

Nutritional Value per Serving: Calories 379, Fat 14.5g, Carbohydrates 36.2g, Protein 34.5g

35.   Spicy Grilled Turkey Legs

Preparation Time: 10 minutes   **Cooking Time:** 1 hour
Servings: 4

Ingredients:
- 4 turkey legs
- 2 tablespoons olive oil
- 1 tablespoon smoked paprika
- 1 tablespoon chili powder
- 1 teaspoon cayenne pepper
- Salt and pepper to taste

Directions: Preheat your grill to medium heat.
Rub the turkey legs with olive oil, then season with smoked paprika, chili powder, cayenne pepper, salt, and pepper.
Grill the turkey legs for about an hour, turning occasionally, until they reach an internal temperature of 180 degrees F.

Nutritional Value per Serving: Calories 363, Fat 15.6g, Carbs 1.8g, Protein 47.4g

---

36.   Lemon and Garlic Grilled Turkey Cutlets

Preparation Time: 10 minutes   **Cooking Time:** 10 minutes
Servings: 4

Ingredients:
- 4 turkey cutlets (about 1 lb)
- Juice of 2 lemons
- 4 garlic cloves, minced
- 2 tablespoons olive oil
- Salt and pepper to taste

Directions: Preheat your grill to medium-high heat.
In a bowl, combine the lemon juice, garlic, olive oil, salt, and pepper. Add the turkey cutlets and let them marinate for about 10 minutes.
Grill the cutlets for about 5 minutes on each side.

Nutritional Value per Serving: Calories 204, Fat 7.8g, Carbs 2.1g, Protein 28.9g

---

37. BBQ Turkey Ribs

Preparation Time: 15 minutes

Cooking Time: 2 hours

Servings: 4

Ingredients:
- *2 lbs turkey ribs*
- *2 cups BBQ sauce*
- *Salt and pepper to taste*

Directions: Preheat your grill to low heat.

Season the turkey ribs with salt and pepper, then slather them with about half of the BBQ sauce.

Grill the ribs, covered, for about 2 hours, or until they're tender and fully cooked. Baste them with the remaining BBQ sauce periodically.

Serve the ribs with extra BBQ sauce on the side, if desired.

Shopping Tips: Turkey ribs might be harder to find than other cuts, but you can ask your butcher to cut them for you.

Nutritional Value per Serving: Calories 468, Fat 10.4g, Carbohydrates 38.8g, Protein 49g

Pork

38.   Sweet and Spicy BBQ Pork Chops

Preparation Time: 15 minutes   **Cooking Time:** 15 minutes
Servings: 4

Ingredients:
- *4 bone-in pork chops*
- *1 cup BBQ sauce*
- *2 tablespoons honey*
- *1 tablespoon hot sauce*
- *Salt and pepper to taste*

Directions: In a bowl, mix the BBQ sauce, honey, hot sauce, salt, and pepper. Reserve 1/4 cup of the sauce for basting.
Marinate the pork chops in the remaining sauce for at least 1 hour, or overnight. Preheat your grill to medium-high heat. Cook the pork chops for about 7 minutes on each side, or when their internal temperature reaches 145°F. Baste with the reserved sauce during the last few minutes of cooking.

Nutritional Value per Serving: Calories 347, Fat 15.6g, Carbohydrates 24.5g, Protein 27.7g

39.   Grilled Pork Tenderloin with Herb Rub

Preparation Time: 15 minutes   **Cooking Time:** 20 minutes
Servings: 4

Ingredients:
- 1 pork tenderloin (about 1 lb)
- 1/4 cup olive oil
- 1 tablespoon fresh rosemary, finely chopped
- 1 tablespoon fresh thyme, finely chopped
- 2 garlic cloves, minced
- Salt and pepper to taste

Directions: In a bowl, mix the olive oil, rosemary, thyme, garlic, salt, and pepper. Rub this mixture all over the pork tenderloin.

Preheat your grill to medium-high heat. Cook the pork tenderloin for about 10 minutes on each side, or until it reaches an internal temperature of 145°F. Let it rest for 5 minutes before slicing.

Shopping Tips: Fresh herbs will give the best flavor in this recipe. If you can't find fresh, you can use dried – just use half the amount.

Nutritional Value per Serving: Calories 254, Fat 14.5g, Carbs 2.1g, Protein 24.3g

---

40.   BBQ Pork Ribs with Brown Sugar Dry Rub

Preparation Time: 20 minutes   **Cooking Time:** 4 hours
Servings: 8

Ingredients:
- 2 racks of pork ribs (about 2 lbs each)
- 1/2 cup brown sugar
- 1/4 cup paprika
- 1 tablespoon black pepper
- 1 tablespoon salt
- 1 tablespoon chili powder
- 1 tablespoon garlic powder
- 1 tablespoon onion powder
- 1 teaspoon cayenne pepper
- 2 cups BBQ sauce

Directions: In a bowl, combine brown sugar, paprika, black pepper, salt, onion powder, chili powder, garlic powder, and cayenne pepper. Rub the mixture all over the pork ribs.

Preheat your grill to low heat. Cook the ribs on the grill, covered, for about 4 hours, or until they're tender and cooked through.

In the last 30 minutes of cooking, baste the ribs with BBQ sauce.

Nutritional Value per Serving: Calories 551, Fat 32.3g, Carbohydrates 34.7g, Protein 28.4g

41.   Grilled Pork Skewers with Pineapple Salsa

Preparation Time: 25 minutes   **Cooking Time:** 15 minutes
Servings: 4

Ingredients:
- 1 lb pork loin, cut into 1-inch cubes
- 1 cup BBQ sauce
- 1 pineapple, diced
- 1 red bell pepper, diced
- 1 jalapeno, minced
- 1/4 cup fresh cilantro, chopped
- 1 lime, juiced
- Salt to taste

Directions: Marinate the pork cubes in the BBQ sauce for at least 1 hour.
Preheat your grill to medium-high heat. Thread the pork onto skewers and grill for about 15 minutes, or until the pork is cooked through.
While the pork is cooking, make the salsa: Combine the pineapple, bell pepper, jalapeno, cilantro, lime juice, and salt in a bowl.
Serve the pork skewers with the pineapple salsa on the side.

Nutritional Value per Serving: Calories 323, Fat 8.6g, Carbohydrates 33.4g, Protein 26.8g

---

42.   Honey Garlic Pork Chops

Preparation Time: 10 minutes   **Cooking Time:** 20 minutes
Servings: 4

Ingredients:
- 4 bone-in pork chops
- 1/4 cup honey
- 4 cloves garlic, minced
- 2 tablespoons soy sauce
- Salt and black pepper to taste

Directions: Mix honey, garlic, soy sauce, salt, and pepper in a bowl to make the marinade.
Marinate the pork chops in the honey garlic sauce for at least an hour.
Preheat your grill to medium-high heat and grill the pork chops for 8-10 minutes on each side or when it reaches a temperature of 145 degrees Fahrenheit inside.

Nutritional Value per Serving: Calories 317, Fat 13.4g, Carbohydrates 18.4g, Protein 30.9g

43.   Grilled Pork Tenderloin with Peach Glaze

Preparation Time: 15 minutes   **Cooking Time:** 20 minutes
Servings: 4

Ingredients:
- 1 pork tenderloin (about 1 lb)
- Salt and pepper to taste
- 1 cup peach preserves
- 1 tablespoon apple cider vinegar
- 1 tablespoon Dijon mustard
- 1 teaspoon minced garlic
- 1/4 teaspoon crushed red pepper flakes

Directions: Season the pork tenderloin with salt and pepper.
In a saucepan, combine the peach preserves, apple cider vinegar, Dijon mustard, garlic, and red pepper flakes. Simmer until the sauce thickens slightly.
Preheat your grill to medium-high heat. Grill the tenderloin for about 20 minutes, or when it reaches a temperature of 145 degrees Fahrenheit inside.
During the last 5 minutes of grilling, baste the tenderloin with the peach glaze.

Nutritional Value per Serving: Calories 378, Fat 6.3g, Carbs 40.8g, Protein 38.6g

---

44.   Citrus-Marinated Pork Shoulder

Preparation Time: 20 minutes (plus marinating time)   **Cooking Time:** 3-4 hours
Servings: 6-8

Ingredients:
- 1 pork shoulder (about 3 lb)
- 4 oranges, juiced
- 2 lemons, juiced
- 4 cloves garlic, minced
- 2 tablespoons olive oil
- Salt and pepper to taste

Directions: In a large bowl, mix together orange juice, lemon juice, minced garlic, olive oil, salt, and pepper.
Add the pork shoulder to the marinade and ensure it's well-coated. Cover and refrigerate for at least 4 hours or overnight.
Preheat your grill to medium-low heat. Cook the pork shoulder, turning occasionally, for about 3-4 hours, or when it reaches a temperature of 195 degrees Fahrenheit inside.

Shopping Tips: When purchasing a pork shoulder, look for one that has a thick layer of fat on one side. This will help to keep the pork moist during the long cooking process.

Nutritional Value per Serving: Calories 452, Fat 28.3g, Carbs 11.4g, Protein 37.9g

45.   Apple-Stuffed Pork Loin

Preparation Time: 30 minutes
Servings: 4-6

Cooking Time: 1 hour

Ingredients:
- 1 pork loin (about 2 lb)
- 2 apples, cored and chopped
- 1/2 cup breadcrumbs
- 1/4 cup brown sugar
- 1 teaspoon cinnamon
- Salt and pepper to taste

Directions: Preheat your grill to medium heat.
In a bowl, combine chopped apples, breadcrumbs, brown sugar, and cinnamon.
Create a pocket on one side of the pork loin and stuff it with the apple mixture. Secure the opening with kitchen twine or toothpicks.
Season the outside of the pork loin with salt and pepper. Grill for about 1 hour, or when it reaches a temperature of 145 degrees Fahrenheit inside.

Shopping Tips: Choose a pork loin that is pinkish-red in color. Also, opt for a firm apple variety that can hold its shape during cooking, such as Granny Smith or Honeycrisp.

Nutritional Value per Serving: Calories 348, Fat 10.6g, Carbohydrates 24.5g, Protein 38.7g

---

46.   Grilled Pork Tenderloin with Pineapple Salsa

Preparation Time: 25 minutes
Servings: 4-6

Cooking Time: 20 minutes

Ingredients:
- 1 pork tenderloin (about 1.5 lb)
- Salt and pepper to taste

For the salsa:
- 1 cup pineapple, diced
- 1 red bell pepper, diced
- 1/4 cup red onion, diced
- 1/4 cup cilantro, chopped
- Juice of 1 lime
- 1 jalapeño, seeded and minced

Directions: Preheat your grill to medium-high heat. Season the pork tenderloin with salt and pepper.
Grill the pork tenderloin for about 20 minutes, turning occasionally, until it reaches an internal temperature of 145 degrees Fahrenheit.

While the pork is grilling, mix together the pineapple, red onion, cilantro, red bell pepper, lime juice, and jalapeño to make the salsa.

Allow the pork to rest for a few minutes after it comes off the grill, then serve with the pineapple salsa.

Shopping Tips: Look for a pork tenderloin that is pinkish-red in color with a minimal amount of fat. Also, choose a ripe pineapple that gives slightly to pressure and has a sweet smell.

Nutritional Value per Serving: Calories 264, Fat 5.3g, Carbs 14.5g, Protein 33.1g

47.　Barbecued Pork Ribs with Homemade Sauce

Preparation Time: 15 minutes　　　　　　　　　**Cooking Time:** 3 hours
Servings: 4-6

Ingredients:
- 2 racks of pork ribs (about 3 lb)
- Salt and pepper to taste

For the sauce:
- 1 cup ketchup
- 1/4 cup apple cider vinegar
- 1/4 cup brown sugar
- 1 tablespoon Worcestershire sauce
- 1 teaspoon smoked paprika
- 1/2 teaspoon garlic powder
- 1/2 teaspoon onion powder

Directions: Preheat your grill to low heat. Season the ribs with salt and pepper.

In a bowl, mix together the ketchup, apple cider vinegar, brown sugar, Worcestershire sauce, smoked paprika, garlic powder, and onion powder to make the barbecue sauce. Grill the ribs over indirect heat for about 3 hours, basting with the barbecue sauce during the last 30 minutes of cooking, until the meat is tender and the internal temperature reaches 145 degrees Fahrenheit.

Shopping Tips: When shopping for pork ribs, look for racks that have even, thick meat coverage over the bones and minimal amounts of fat.

Nutritional Value per Serving: Calories 503, Fat 28.7g, Carbohydrates 25.6g, Protein 38.9g

Fish and Seafood

48.   Honey Lime Grilled Salmon

Preparation Time: 15 minutes   **Cooking Time:** 15 minutes
Servings: 4

Ingredients:
- *4 salmon fillets (6 oz each)*
- *1/4 cup honey*
- *Juice of 2 limes*
- *2 cloves garlic, minced*
- *Salt and pepper to taste*

Directions: In a bowl, combine honey, lime juice, and garlic. Season the salmon with salt and pepper and coat with the honey-lime mixture.
Preheat the grill to medium heat. Place the salmon on the grill and cook for 5-7 minutes per side, or until the fish flakes easily with a fork.

Shopping Tips: Look for salmon fillets with bright, moist skin.

Nutritional Value per Serving: Calories 342, Fat 13.6g, Carbohydrates 26.1g, Protein 34.6g

49. Grilled Mahi Mahi with Mango Salsa

Preparation Time: 20 minutes   **Cooking Time:** 10 minutes
Servings: 4

Ingredients:
- 4 mahi mahi fillets (6 oz each)
- Salt and pepper to taste

For the mango salsa:
- 1 mango, diced
- 1/4 cup red onion, diced
- 1/4 cup cilantro, chopped
- Juice of 1 lime

Directions: Season the mahi mahi fillets with salt and pepper. Preheat the grill to medium heat. Grill the mahi mahi for about 5 minutes per side. While the fish is grilling, mix together the cilantro, mango, lime juice, and red onion to make the salsa. Serve the fish with the mango salsa on top.

Nutritional Value per Serving: Calories 254, Fat 1.3g, Carbohydrates 16.8g, Protein 38.2g

---

50. Grilled Lemon-Pepper Tuna Steaks

Preparation Time: 10 minutes   **Cooking Time:** 10 minutes
Servings: 4

Ingredients:
- 4 tuna steaks (6 oz each)
- 2 lemons, juiced
- 1 tablespoon of olive oil
- 2 teaspoons of freshly ground black pepper
- Salt to taste

Directions: In a large dish, mix the lemon juice, olive oil, black pepper, and salt. Place the tuna steaks in the marinade and turn to coat. Let them marinate for 10 minutes. Preheat your grill to high heat. Grill the tuna steaks for about 3-4 minutes per side.

Nutritional Value per Serving: Calories 214, Fat 5.3g, Carbohydrates 2.2g, Protein 37.8g

51. Grilled Swordfish with Herb Butter

Preparation Time: 10 minutes   **Cooking Time:** 10 minutes
Servings: 4

Ingredients:

- 4 swordfish steaks (6 oz each)
- 1/4 cup butter, softened
- 2 tablespoons of fresh herbs (such as parsley, thyme, and oregano), chopped
- Salt and pepper to taste

Directions: Preheat your grill to medium heat. Season the swordfish steaks with salt and pepper.
In a small bowl, mix together the softened butter and chopped herbs. Set aside.
Grill the swordfish for about 4-5 minutes per side. Just before serving, place a spoonful of the herb butter on top of each steak.

Nutritional Value per Serving: Calories 303, Fat 17.6g, Carbohydrates 1.4g, Protein 34.3g

---

52. Grilled Shrimp Skewers with Garlic-Lime Marinade

Preparation Time: 15 minutes (plus 30 minutes marinating time)
Cooking Time: 5 minutes   **Servings:** 4

Ingredients:

- 1 lb large shrimp, peeled and deveined
- Juice of 2 limes
- 4 cloves garlic, minced
- Salt and pepper to taste
- 8 skewers

Directions: In a bowl, combine the lime juice, minced garlic, salt, and pepper. Add the shrimp and toss to coat. Let the shrimp marinate for about 30 minutes in the fridge.
Preheat your grill to high heat. Thread the shrimp onto skewers.
Grill the skewers for about 2-3 minutes per side, or until the shrimp are cooked through.

Nutritional Value per Serving: Calories 147, Fat 1.8g, Carbohydrates 3.2g, Protein 24.5g

53. Grilled Lobster Tails with Garlic Butter

Preparation Time: 15 minutes   **Cooking Time:** 10 minutes
Servings: 4

Ingredients:
- 4 lobster tails, halved lengthwise
- 1/2 cup butter
- 4 cloves garlic, minced
- Salt and pepper to taste

Directions: Preheat your grill to high heat. Season the lobster tails with salt and pepper.
In a small saucepan, melt the butter over medium heat. Add the minced garlic and cook until fragrant, about 1-2 minutes.
Place the lobster tails - meat side down - on the grill, and cook for about 4-5 minutes. Flip the tails over and brush them with the garlic butter. Continue grilling for another 5-6 minutes, or until the lobster meat is opaque and cooked through.

Nutritional Value per Serving: Calories 332, Fat 23.4g, Carbohydrates 1.8g, Protein 28.2g

54. Grilled Scallops with Lemon Herb Sauce

Preparation Time: 10 minutes   **Cooking Time:** 10 minutes
Servings: 4

Ingredients:
- 1 lb scallops
- Salt and pepper to taste

For the lemon herb sauce:
- 2 lemons, juiced
- 1/4 cup olive oil
- 1 tablespoon of fresh herbs (such as parsley, thyme, and dill), chopped

Directions: Preheat your grill to medium-high heat. Season the scallops with salt and pepper. In a small bowl, whisk together the lemon juice, olive oil, and chopped herbs. Grill the scallops for about 2-3 minutes per side, or until they are opaque and cooked through. Drizzle the scallops with the lemon herb sauce just before serving.

Nutritional Value per Serving: Calories 211, Fat 14.6g, Carbohydrates 6.7g, Protein 14.3g

55.   Grilled Oysters with Spicy Butter

Preparation Time: 15 minutes   **Cooking Time:** 10 minutes
Servings: 4

Ingredients:
- *12 oysters, scrubbed clean*
- *1/4 cup butter, softened*
- *1 jalapeno pepper, seeds removed and finely chopped*
- *Salt to taste*

Directions: Preheat your grill to medium heat.
In a small bowl, mix together the chopped jalapeno and softened butter. Set aside. Place the oysters (shell side down) on the grill. Cook until the shells start to open, (about 5-10 minutes). Carefully remove the top shell from each oyster, then top each one with a spoonful of the spicy butter. Continue grilling for another 2-3 minutes, or until the butter is melted and bubbly.

Nutritional Value per Serving: Calories 176, Fat 12.4g, Carbohydrates 6.2g, Protein 8.6g

56.   Grilled Clams with Herb Butter

Preparation Time: 15 minutes   **Cooking Time:** 10 minutes
Servings: 4

Ingredients:
- *2 lbs clams, scrubbed clean*
- *1/4 cup butter, softened*
- *2 tablespoons of fresh herbs (such as parsley and thyme), chopped*
- *Salt and pepper to taste*

Directions: Preheat your grill to medium heat.
In a small bowl, mix together the chopped herbs, softened butter, salt, and pepper. Place the clams directly on the grill grates. Grill for about 5-10 minutes, or until the clams open up. Discard clams that do not open. Spoon the herb butter into each open clam.

Nutritional Value per Serving: Calories 209, Fat 12.1g, Carbohydrates 8.3g, Protein 16.4g

57. Grilled Mussels with Garlic-Lemon Butter

Preparation Time: 20 minutes

Cooking Time: 10 minutes

Servings: 4

Ingredients:

- 2 lbs mussels, scrubbed and debearded
- 1/4 cup butter
- 4 cloves garlic, minced
- 1 lemon, juiced
- Salt and pepper to taste

Directions: Preheat your grill to medium heat.

In a small saucepan, melt the butter over medium heat. Add the minced garlic and cook until fragrant, about 1-2 minutes. Remove from the heat and stir in the lemon juice, salt, and pepper.

Grill the mussels for about 5-10 minutes, or until the shells open. Discard any mussels that do not open. Drizzle the mussels with the garlic-lemon butter just before serving.

Nutritional Value per Serving: Calories 217, Fat 12.8g, Carbohydrates 10.1g, Protein 18.7g

Vegetables

58.   Grilled Zucchini with Parmesan

Preparation Time: 10 minutes

Cooking Time: 10 minutes

Servings: 4

Ingredients:
- 4 medium zucchinis, sliced lengthwise into halves
- 1/4 cup olive oil
- Salt and pepper to taste
- 2 tablespoons of fresh herbs (such as rosemary and thyme), chopped
- 1/2 cup grated Parmesan cheese

Directions: Preheat your grill to medium heat. Brush the zucchini halves with olive oil and season with salt, pepper, and herbs.

Grill the zucchini, cut side down, for about 5 minutes. Flip the zucchini over and sprinkle with the Parmesan cheese. Grill for another 5 minutes.

Shopping Tips: Look for zucchinis that are firm, have a vibrant green color, and are small to medium-sized for the best flavor and texture.

Nutritional Value per Serving: Calories 198, Fat 15.2g, Carbohydrates 7.8g, Protein 7.2g

59.   Grilled Corn on the Cob with Garlic Herb Butter

Preparation Time: 15 minutes   **Cooking Time:** 15 minutes
Servings: 4

Ingredients:
- 4 ears of corn, husks and silks removed
- 1/4 cup butter, softened
- 2 cloves garlic, minced
- 2 tablespoons of fresh herbs (such as parsley and chives), chopped
- Salt and pepper to taste

Directions: Preheat your grill to medium heat.
In a small bowl, combine the softened butter, minced garlic, chopped herbs, salt, and pepper.
Grill the corn, turning occasionally, for about 15 minutes. Remove from the grill and immediately slather each ear of corn with the garlic herb butter.

Nutritional Value per Serving: Calories 211, Fat 12.3g, Carbohydrates 27.6g, Protein 4.2g

60.   Grilled Portobello Mushrooms with Balsamic Glaze

Preparation Time: 10 minutes   **Cooking Time:** 15 minutes
Servings: 4

Ingredients:
- 4 large Portobello mushrooms, stems removed
- 1/4 cup olive oil
- Salt and pepper to taste
- 1/4 cup balsamic vinegar
- 2 cloves garlic, minced

Directions: Preheat your grill to medium heat. Brush the mushrooms with olive oil and season with salt and pepper.
In a small saucepan, combine the balsamic vinegar and minced garlic. Bring to a simmer over medium heat and cook until the vinegar is reduced by half, about 5 minutes. Set aside.
Grill the mushrooms for about 7 minutes on each side, or until tender and lightly charred. Remove from the grill and drizzle with the balsamic glaze.

Nutritional Value per Serving: Calories 177, Fat 14.4g, Carbohydrates 10.6g, Protein 3.2g

61.   Grilled Asparagus with Lemon and Parmesan

Preparation Time: 10 minutes   **Cooking Time:** 10 minutes
Servings: 4

Ingredients:

- *1 lb asparagus, trimmed*
- *2 tablespoons olive oil*
- *Salt and pepper to taste*
- *Zest and juice of 1 lemon*
- *1/4 cup grated Parmesan cheese*

Directions: Preheat your grill to medium heat. Toss the asparagus in olive oil, salt, and pepper.
Grill the asparagus for about 5 minutes on each side, or until tender and lightly charred. Remove from the grill and sprinkle with the lemon juice, lemon zest, and grated Parmesan.

Nutritional Value per Serving: Calories 131, Fat 10.4g, Carbohydrates 6.2g, Protein 5.7g

---

62.   Sweet Corn on the Cob with Lime and Chili Butter

Preparation Time: 10 minutes   **Cooking Time:** 15 minutes
Servings: 6

Ingredients:

- *6 ears of corn, husked*
- *1/2 cup unsalted butter, room temperature*
- *Zest and juice of 1 lime*
- *1 teaspoon chili powder*
- *Salt and pepper to taste*

Directions: Preheat your grill to medium heat.
In a bowl, mix the butter, lime zest, lime juice, and chili powder. Season with salt and pepper.
Grill the corn for about 15 minutes, turning occasionally, until tender and charred.
Serve the corn with the chili-lime butter on top.

Nutritional Value per Serving: Calories 223, Fat 15.4g, Carbohydrates 21.3g, Protein 3.2g

63.   **Charred Bell Peppers with Goat Cheese**

Preparation Time: 10 minutes   **Cooking Time:** 15 minutes
Servings: 4

Ingredients:
- *4 bell peppers, any color*
- *2 tablespoons olive oil*
- *Salt and pepper to taste*
- *1 cup goat cheese, crumbled*

Directions: Preheat your grill to medium heat. Slice the peppers in half lengthwise and remove the seeds. Brush with olive oil and season with salt and pepper.
Grill the peppers for about 7 minutes on each side, until softened and charred. Remove from the grill and fill each pepper half with crumbled goat cheese.

Nutritional Value per Serving: Calories 246, Fat 19.2g, Carbohydrates 14.2g, Protein 9.8g

---

64.   **Grilled Zucchini Ribbons with Pesto and Pine Nuts**

Preparation Time: 15 minutes   **Cooking Time:** 10 minutes
Servings: 4

Ingredients:
- *4 zucchinis*
- *2 tablespoons olive oil*
- *Salt and pepper to taste*
- *1/4 cup basil pesto*
- *1/4 cup pine nuts, toasted*

Directions: Preheat your grill to medium heat. Slice the zucchinis lengthwise into thin ribbons using a vegetable peeler. Toss with olive oil, salt, and pepper.
Grill the zucchini ribbons for 1-2 minutes on each side, until tender and lightly charred. Remove from the grill and drizzle with the pesto. Sprinkle with toasted pine nuts.

Shopping Tips: Look for small to medium-sized zucchinis that are firm and have shiny skin.

Nutritional Value per Serving: Calories 183, Fat 15.7g, Carbohydrates 11.3g, Protein 4.5g

65.   Grilled Eggplant with Tomato and Feta

Preparation Time: 10 minutes   **Cooking Time:** 15 minutes
Servings: 4

Ingredients:
- 2 large eggplants
- 2 tablespoons olive oil
- Salt and pepper to taste
- 2 tomatoes, sliced
- 1/4 cup fresh basil leaves
- 1/2 cup feta cheese, crumbled

Directions: Preheat your grill to medium heat. Slice the eggplants into 1/2-inch thick rounds. Brush both sides with olive oil and season with salt and pepper.
Grill the eggplant for about 5-7 minutes on each side, until tender and lightly charred.
Top each eggplant round with a few basil leaves, a slice of tomato, and a dusting of feta cheese.

Nutritional Value per Serving: Calories 203, Fat 12.6g, Carbohydrates 20.3g, Protein 7.1g

---

66.   Grilled Artichokes with Garlic-Lemon Aioli

Preparation Time: 15 minutes   **Cooking Time:** 30 minutes
Servings: 4

Ingredients:
- 4 artichokes
- 2 lemons, halved
- 1/2 cup mayonnaise
- 2 cloves garlic, minced
- Salt and pepper to taste

Directions: Preheat your grill to medium heat. Cut the artichokes in half lengthwise and squeeze lemon juice over the cut surfaces to keep the artichokes from browning.
Grill the artichokes cut side down for about 15 minutes, then flip and grill for another 15 minutes, until tender.
In a small bowl, mix the minced garlic, mayonnaise, and the juice of the remaining lemons. Season with salt and pepper.
Serve the artichokes with the garlic-lemon aioli for dipping.

Shopping Tips: Look for artichokes that have tight, compact leaves and feel heavy for their size.

Nutritional Value per Serving: Calories 288, Fat 22.2g, Carbohydrates 23.4g, Protein 7.6g

67. Maple-Glazed Butternut Squash

Preparation Time: 15 minutes   **Cooking Time:** 20 minutes
Servings: 4

Ingredients:
- *1 large butternut squash*
- *2 tablespoons olive oil*
- *Salt and pepper to taste*
- *1/4 cup maple syrup*
- *1/4 teaspoon cayenne pepper*

Directions: Preheat your grill to medium heat. Peel the butternut squash and slice into 1/2-inch thick rounds. Toss with olive oil, salt, and pepper.
In a small bowl, mix the maple syrup and cayenne pepper.
Grill the squash for about 10 minutes on each side. Brush with the maple glaze during the last few minutes of grilling.

Shopping Tips: Choose butternut squash that is heavy for its size with a hard, unblemished skin.

Nutritional Value per Serving: Calories 217, Fat 7.6g, Carbohydrates 40.2g, Protein 2.2g

Rubs, Sauce and Marinades

68.   Sweet and Spicy BBQ Rub

Preparation Time: 10 minutes

Yield: Approximately 1.5 cups

Ingredients:

- 1/2 cup brown sugar
- 1/4 cup paprika
- 1 tablespoon black pepper
- 1 tablespoon salt
- 1 tablespoon chili powder
- 1 tablespoon garlic powder
- 1 tablespoon onion powder
- 1 teaspoon cayenne pepper

Directions: In a bowl, mix together all the ingredients until well combined. Store in an airtight container until ready to use. Rub should be applied to meat 30 minutes before grilling.

Nutritional Value per Serving (1 tablespoon): Calories 27, Fat 0.52g, Carbohydrates 7.3g, Protein 0.4g

69. Coffee-Chili Rub

Description: This robust rub is perfect for beef, adding a rich and earthy flavor with a hint of heat.

Preparation Time: 10 minutes   **Yield:** Approximately 3/4 cup

Ingredients:
- 2 tablespoons finely ground coffee
- 2 tablespoons brown sugar
- 2 tablespoons chili powder
- 1 tablespoon paprika
- 1 tablespoon cumin
- 1 tablespoon salt
- 1 teaspoon black pepper
- 1 teaspoon cayenne pepper

Directions: In a bowl, mix together all the ingredients until well combined. Store in an airtight container until ready to use. Rub should be applied to meat 30 minutes before grilling.

Nutritional Value per Serving (1 tablespoon): Calories 27, Fat 0.48g, Carbohydrates 5.3g, Protein 0.39g

---

70. Lemon-Pepper Rub

Description: A bright and peppery rub that's excellent on chicken and fish.

Preparation Time: 10 minutes   **Yield:** Approximately 1/2 cup

Ingredients:
- Zest of 2 lemons
- 1/4 cup black pepper
- 1/4 cup salt
- 1 tablespoon garlic powder
- 1 tablespoon onion powder

Directions: In a bowl, mix together all the ingredients until well combined. Store in an airtight container until ready to use. Rub should be applied to meat 30 minutes before grilling.

Nutritional Value per Serving (1 tablespoon): Calories 9.6, Fat 0g, Carbohydrates 2.1g, Protein 0.53g

---

71.   Herb and Garlic Rub

Description: This versatile rub adds a punch of flavor to everything from vegetables to any kind of meat.

Preparation Time: 10 minutes   **Yield:** Approximately 1 cup

Ingredients:
- 1/4 cup dried basil
- 1/4 cup dried oregano
- 1/4 cup garlic powder
- 1 tablespoon salt
- 1 tablespoon black pepper

Directions: In a bowl, mix together all the ingredients until well combined. Store in an airtight container until ready to use. Rub should be applied to food 30 minutes before grilling.

Nutritional Value per Serving (1 tablespoon): Calories 18, Fat 0.3g, Carbohydrates 4.1g, Protein 1.5g

---

72.   Cajun Spice Rub

Description: This Cajun rub adds a Southern twist to your grilling, great for shrimp, chicken, and fish.

Preparation Time: 10 minutes   **Yield:** Approximately 1 cup

Ingredients:
- 1/4 cup paprika
- 1/4 cup garlic powder
- 2 tablespoons onion powder
- 2 tablespoons dried thyme
- 1 tablespoon salt
- 1 tablespoon black pepper
- 1 tablespoon cayenne pepper

Directions: In a bowl, mix together all the ingredients until well combined. Store in an airtight container until ready to use. Rub should be applied to food 30 minutes before grilling.

Nutritional Value per Serving (1 tablespoon): Calories 23, Fat 0.36g, Carbohydrates 3.4g, Protein 1g

Please remember to store all these rubs in a cool, dark place for up to six months.

73.   **Classic BBQ Sauce**

Description: A sweet and tangy sauce that's perfect for any grilled meat.

Preparation Time: 10 minutes   **Cooking Time:** 20 minutes
Yield: Approximately 2 cups

Ingredients:
- 1 cup ketchup
- 1/2 cup apple cider vinegar
- 1/2 cup brown sugar
- 2 tablespoons Worcestershire sauce
- 2 tablespoons mustard
- 1 teaspoon smoked paprika
- 1 teaspoon garlic powder
- 1/2 teaspoon black pepper
- 1/2 teaspoon salt

Directions: In a saucepan, combine all ingredients.
Bring to a simmer over medium heat and cook, stirring occasionally, for about 20 minutes or until the sauce has thickened to your desired consistency.
Allow the sauce to cool before using, or store in an airtight container in the fridge for up to a week.

Nutritional Value per Serving (2 tablespoons): Calories 69, Fat 0g, Carbohydrates 17.2g, Protein 0g

---

74.   **Honey Mustard Sauce**

Description: This sweet and tangy sauce is perfect for chicken or as a dipping sauce.

Preparation Time: 10 minutes   **Yield:** Approximately 1 cup

Ingredients:
- 1/2 cup mayonnaise
- 2 tablespoons honey
- 2 tablespoons Dijon mustard
- 1 tablespoon white vinegar
- 1/4 teaspoon salt

Directions: In a bowl, mix together all the ingredients until smooth.
Use right away or keep in the refrigerator in an airtight container. for up to a week.

Nutritional Value per Serving (2 tablespoons): Calories 107, Fat 9.4g, Carbohydrates 7.2g, Protein 0g

75. Spicy BBQ Sauce

Description: This sauce has a kick to it and pairs well with beef and pork.

Preparation Time: 10 minutes   **Cooking Time:** 20 minutes
Yield: Approximately 2 cups

Ingredients:
- 1 cup ketchup
- 1/4 cup apple cider vinegar
- 1/4 cup brown sugar
- 2 tablespoons hot sauce
- 1 tablespoon Worcestershire sauce
- 1 teaspoon onion powder
- 1 teaspoon garlic powder
- 1/2 teaspoon black pepper
- 1/2 teaspoon salt

Directions: In a saucepan, combine all ingredients.
Bring to a simmer over medium heat and cook, stirring occasionally, for about 20 minutes or until the sauce has thickened to your desired consistency.
Allow the sauce to cool before using, or store in an airtight container in the fridge for up to a week.

Nutritional Value per Serving (2 tablespoons): Calories 72, Fat 0g, Carbohydrates 17.4g, Protein 0g

---

76. Classic BBQ Sauce

Description: A sweet and tangy sauce that's perfect for any grilled meat.

Preparation Time: 10 minutes   **Cooking Time:** 20 minutes
Yield: Approximately 2 cups

Ingredients:
- 1 cup ketchup
- 1/2 cup apple cider vinegar
- 1/2 cup brown sugar
- 2 tablespoons Worcestershire sauce
- 2 tablespoons mustard
- 1 teaspoon smoked paprika
- 1 teaspoon garlic powder
- 1/2 teaspoon black pepper
- 1/2 teaspoon salt

Directions: In a saucepan, combine all ingredients.
Bring to a simmer over medium heat and cook, stirring occasionally, for about 20 minutes or until the sauce has thickened to your desired consistency.
Allow the sauce to cool before using, or store in an airtight container in the fridge for up to a week.

Nutritional Value per Serving (2 tablespoons): Calories 76, Fat 0g, Carbohydrates 17.5g, Protein 0g

77. **Honey Mustard Sauce**

Description: This sweet and tangy sauce is perfect for chicken or as a dipping sauce.

Preparation Time: 10 minutes   **Yield:** Approximately 1 cup

Ingredients:
- *1/2 cup mayonnaise*
- *2 tablespoons honey*
- *2 tablespoons Dijon mustard*
- *1 tablespoon white vinegar*
- *1/4 teaspoon salt*

Directions: In a bowl, mix together all the ingredients until smooth.
Use immediately, or store in an airtight container in the fridge for up to a week.

Nutritional Value per Serving (2 tablespoons): Calories 110, Fat 9g, Carbohydrates 7g, Protein 0g

---

78. **Spicy BBQ Sauce**

Description: This sauce has a kick to it and pairs well with beef and pork.

Preparation Time: 10 minutes   **Cooking Time:** 20 minutes
Yield: Approximately 2 cups

Ingredients:
- *1 cup ketchup*
- *1/4 cup apple cider vinegar*
- *1/4 cup brown sugar*
- *2 tablespoons hot sauce*
- *1 tablespoon Worcestershire sauce*
- *1 teaspoon onion powder*
- *1 teaspoon garlic powder*
- *1/2 teaspoon black pepper*
- *1/2 teaspoon salt*

Directions: In a saucepan, combine all ingredients.
Bring to a simmer over medium heat and cook, stirring occasionally, for about 20 minutes or until the sauce has thickened to your desired consistency.
Allow the sauce to cool before using, or store in an airtight container in the fridge for up to a week.

Nutritional Value per Serving (2 tablespoons): Calories 72, Fat 0g, Carbohydrates 17.1g, Protein 0g

79.   Teriyaki Sauce

Description: A sweet and salty sauce that's perfect for grilling chicken, beef, and fish.

Preparation Time: 10 minutes   **Cooking Time**: 20 minutes
Yield: Approximately 1 cup

Ingredients:
- *1/2 cup soy sauce*
- *1/2 cup mirin (sweet rice wine)*
- *1/4 cup brown sugar*
- *2 cloves garlic, minced*
- *1 teaspoon grated fresh ginger*

Directions:
In a saucepan, combine all ingredients.
Bring to a simmer over medium heat and cook, stirring occasionally, for about 20 minutes or until the sauce has thickened to your desired consistency.
Allow the sauce to cool before using, or store in an airtight container in the fridge for up to a week.

Nutritional Value per Serving (2 tablespoons): Calories 66, Fat 0g, Carbohydrates 15.6g, Protein 2.3g

---

80.   Chimichurri Sauce

Description: A fresh and tangy sauce that's perfect for grilled beef and vegetables.

Preparation Time: 15 minutes   **Yield**: Approximately 1 cup

Ingredients:
- *1 cup fresh parsley, finely chopped*
- *4 cloves garlic, minced*
- *1/2 cup olive oil*
- *1/4 cup red wine vinegar*
- *1 teaspoon dried oregano*
- *1/2 teaspoon red pepper flakes*
- *Salt and pepper to taste*

Directions:
In a bowl, mix together all the ingredients until well combined.
Use immediately, or store in an airtight container in the fridge for up to a week.

Nutritional Value per Serving (2 tablespoons): Calories 117, Fat 13.4g, Carbohydrates 1.1g, Protein 0g

81. Classic BBQ Marinade

Description: Perfect for any grilled meat, this marinade imparts a sweet, smoky flavor.

Preparation Time: 10 minutes   **Yield**: Approximately 2 cups

Ingredients:
- 1 cup BBQ sauce
- 1/4 cup apple cider vinegar
- 1/4 cup honey
- 1/4 cup olive oil
- 2 cloves garlic, minced
- 1 teaspoon smoked paprika
- 1/2 teaspoon black pepper
- 1/2 teaspoon salt

Directions:
In a bowl, mix together all the ingredients until well combined.
Use immediately, or store in an airtight container in the fridge for up to a week.

Nutritional Value per Serving (2 tablespoons): Calories 67, Fat 3.4g, Carbohydrates 9.6g, Protein 0g

82. Lemon-Garlic Marinade

Description: This zesty marinade is perfect for fish, chicken, or vegetables.

Preparation Time: 10 minutes   **Yield**: Approximately 1 cup

Ingredients:
- 1/2 cup olive oil
- 1/4 cup lemon juice
- 4 cloves garlic, minced
- 1 tablespoon fresh rosemary, chopped
- 1 teaspoon lemon zest
- Salt and pepper to taste

Directions:
In a bowl, mix together all the ingredients until well combined.
Use immediately, or store in an airtight container in the fridge for up to a week.

Nutritional Value per Serving (2 tablespoons): Calories 118, Fat 14.2g, Carbohydrates 0.8g, Protein 0g

83. Spicy Asian Marinade

Description: This marinade adds a kick to beef, chicken, or tofu.

Preparation Time: 10 minutes   **Yield**: Approximately 1 cup

Ingredients:
- *1/2 cup soy sauce*
- *1/4 cup sesame oil*
- *2 tablespoons honey*
- *2 cloves garlic, minced*
- *1 tablespoon fresh ginger, minced*
- *1 tablespoon Sriracha sauce*

Directions:
In a bowl, mix together all the ingredients until well combined.
Use immediately, or store in an airtight container in the fridge for up to a week.

Nutritional Value per Serving (2 tablespoons): Calories 83, Fat 7.1g, Carbohydrates 3.4g, Protein 1g

---

84. Herb Marinade

Description: This fresh, herbaceous marinade is perfect for chicken or vegetables.

Preparation Time: 10 minutes   **Yield**: Approximately 1 cup

Ingredients:
- *1/2 cup olive oil*
- *1/4 cup white wine vinegar*
- *1/4 cup fresh parsley, chopped*
- *2 tablespoons fresh basil, chopped*
- *2 cloves garlic, minced*
- *Salt and pepper to taste*

Directions:
In a bowl, mix together all the ingredients until well combined.
Use immediately, or store in an airtight container in the fridge for up to a week.

Nutritional Value per Serving (2 tablespoons): Calories 116, Fat 14.1g, Carbohydrates 1.1g, Protein 0g

85. Sweet and Smoky Marinade

Description: This marinade adds a sweet, smoky flavor to pork or chicken.

Preparation Time: 10 minutes   **Yield**: Approximately 1 cup

Ingredients:
- *1/2 cup brown sugar*
- *1/4 cup smoked paprika*
- *1/4 cup apple cider vinegar*
- *1/4 cup olive oil*
- *2 cloves garlic, minced*
- *Salt and pepper to taste*

Directions:

In a bowl, mix together all the ingredients until well combined.

Use immediately, or store in an airtight container in the fridge for up to a week.

Nutritional Value per Serving (2 tablespoons): Calories 101, Fat 7.6g, Carbohydrates 9.1g, Protein 0g

Desserts

86.   Grilled Pineapple with Honey-Cinnamon Glaze

Preparation Time: 10 minutes   **Cooking Time**: 10 minutes
Servings: 4

Ingredients:
- *1 ripe pineapple*
- *1/4 cup honey*
- *1 teaspoon cinnamon*
- *1/2 teaspoon vanilla extract*

Directions: Preheat the grill to medium-high heat.
Peel the pineapple and cut into rings or spears.
In a small bowl, mix together the honey, cinnamon, and vanilla extract.
Brush the pineapple with the honey mixture.
Grill for about 5 minutes on each side, until caramelized and slightly charred.

Nutritional Value per Serving: Calories 175, Fat 0g, Carbohydrates 47.3g, Protein 1.2g

87.   Grilled Peaches with Vanilla Ice Cream

Preparation Time: 10 minutes   **Cooking Time**: 10 minutes
Servings: 4

Ingredients:
- 4 ripe peaches
- 2 tablespoons brown sugar
- 1 tablespoon butter, melted
- Vanilla ice cream

Directions: Preheat the grill to medium-high heat.
Halves the peaches and remove the pits.
In a small bowl, mix together the brown sugar and melted butter.
Brush the cut side of the peaches with the butter mixture.
Grill cut-side down for about 5 minutes, until caramelized.
Add a scoop of vanilla ice cream to serve.

Nutritional Value per Serving: Calories 183 (excluding ice cream), Fat 3.6g, Carbohydrates 37.2g, Protein 2.1g

---

88.   Grilled Banana Split

Preparation Time: 5 minutes   **Cooking Time**: 10 minutes
Servings: 4

Ingredients:
- 4 ripe bananas
- 1 cup of your favorite ice cream
- Chocolate syrup
- 1/2 cup crushed walnuts
- Whipped cream

Directions: Preheat the grill to medium heat.
Slice the bananas in half lengthwise. Leave the skin on.
Grill cut-side down for about 3-4 minutes, until grill marks appear.
Flip and cook on the skin side for another 3-4 minutes.
Allow to cool slightly, then remove the banana from the skin.
Top with a scoop of ice cream, crushed walnuts, chocolate syrup, and whipped cream.

Nutritional Value per Serving (excluding toppings): Calories 122, Fat 0g, Carbohydrates 31.4g, Protein 1g

89.   Grilled Berries with Sweet Cream

Preparation Time: 10 minutes   **Cooking Time**: 5 minutes
Servings: 4

Ingredients:
- 2 cups mixed berries (such as strawberries, blueberries, raspberries)
- 1/4 cup powdered sugar
- 1 cup heavy cream
- 1/2 teaspoon vanilla extract

Directions: Preheat the grill to medium heat.
Mix the berries with 2 tablespoons of the powdered sugar.
Place the berries in a grill basket or on a piece of foil with holes poked in it.
Grill for about 5 minutes, until the berries are warm and beginning to burst.
While the berries are grilling, whip the heavy cream with the vanilla extract and remaining powdered sugar.
Serve the grilled berries topped with a dollop of the sweet cream.

Nutritional Value per Serving: Calories 222, Fat 11.1g, Carbohydrates 30.3g, Protein 2.4g

---

90.   Chocolate Cookies S'mores

Preparation Time: 5 minutes   **Cooking Time**: 5 minutes
Servings: 4

Ingredients:
- 8 chocolate chip cookies
- 4 marshmallows
- 4 squares of chocolate

Directions: Preheat the grill to low heat.
Place 4 of the cookies bottom-side up on a piece of foil.
Top each cookie with a marshmallow and a square of chocolate.
Top with the remaining cookies.
Wrap the s'mores in the foil and grill for about 5 minutes, until the chocolate and marshmallows are melted.
Let cool for a few minutes before serving.

Nutritional Value per Serving (varies depending on cookies used): Calories 248, Fat 10.4g, Carbohydrates 38.3g, Protein 3.8g

91.   Grilled Apple Crisp Foil Packets

Preparation Time: 10 minutes   **Cooking Time**: 20 minutes
Servings: 4

Ingredients:
- 4 apples
- 1/4 cup brown sugar
- 1/4 cup old-fashioned oats
- 1/4 cup flour
- 4 tablespoons butter
- 1/2 teaspoon cinnamon
- Vanilla ice cream, for serving

Directions: Preheat the grill to medium heat.
Slice the apples and divide them between 4 pieces of foil.
In a small bowl, mix together the brown sugar, oats, flour, and cinnamon.
Cut the butter into small pieces and mix it into the oat mixture until it is crumbly.
Top the apples with the oat mixture.
Fold the foil over the apples to make a packet.
Grill until the apples are tender (about 20 minutes).
Add a scoop of vanilla ice cream to serve.

Nutritional Value per Serving (excluding ice cream): Calories 326, Fat 12.4g, Carbohydrates 54.2g, Protein 3.1g

---

92.   Grilled Cherry Clafoutis

Preparation Time: 15 minutes   **Cooking Time**: 25 minutes
Servings: 4

Ingredients:
- 2 cups fresh cherries, pitted
- 1/2 cup all-purpose flour
- 1/4 cup granulated sugar
- Pinch of salt
- 3 eggs
- 1 cup milk
- 1 teaspoon vanilla extract
- Powdered sugar, for dusting

Directions: Preheat the grill to medium heat.
Scatter the cherries in the bottom of a cast-iron skillet.
In a bowl, whisk together the flour, sugar, and salt.
In another bowl, whisk together the eggs, milk, and vanilla extract.
Gradually combine the wet ingredients and dry ingredients, whisking until smooth.
Pour the batter over the cherries in the skillet.

Cover the grill and cook for about 25 minutes.
Let cool for a few minutes, then dust with powdered sugar before serving.

Nutritional Value per Serving: Calories 231, Fat 5.4g, Carbohydrates 39.8g, Protein 9.1g

---

93.   Grilled Strawberry Shortcake Kebabs

Preparation Time: 10 minutes   **Cooking Time**: 5 minutes
Servings: 4

Ingredients:
- *1 pound strawberries*
- *1 store-bought pound cake*
- *1/2 cup whipped cream*
- *Chocolate syrup, for drizzling*

Directions: Preheat the grill to medium heat.
Cut the strawberries and pound cake into bite-sized pieces.
Thread the strawberries and pound cake onto skewers.
Grill for about 5 minutes, turning occasionally, until grill marks appear.
Serve with some whipped cream and a drizzle of chocolate syrup.

Nutritional Value per Serving (excluding toppings): Calories 345, Fat 9.7g, Carbohydrates 63.2g, Protein 5.3g

Recipes from the World

Argentine Recipes

94.   Argentine Asado Ribs with Chimichurri Sauce

Preparation Time: 1 hour (includes marinating time)
Cooking Time: 1.5-2 hours   **Servings:** 4

Ingredients:
- Ribs (Pork or Beef) - 2 racks
- Salt - to taste
- Pepper - to taste
- Paprika - 1 tsp
- Garlic Cloves - 4, finely chopped
- Olive Oil - 2 tbsp

For the Chimichurri Sauce:
- Parsley - 1 cup, finely chopped
- Oregano - 1/4 cup, finely chopped
- Garlic Cloves - 4, minced
- Red Wine Vinegar - 1/2 cup
- Red Pepper Flakes - 1 tsp
- Olive Oil - 1 cup
- Salt - to taste
- Pepper - to taste

Directions:
In a small bowl, combine the finely chopped parsley, minced garlic, oregano, red pepper flakes, olive oil, salt, red wine vinegar, and pepper to make the sauce. Set aside for at least an hour.
Season the ribs with salt, pepper, paprika, chopped garlic, and olive oil. Let it marinate for at least 30 minutes.
Preheat the barbecue grill to medium heat.
Place the ribs on the grill, bone side down. Grill for about 1.5 to 2 hours.
Serve the ribs with the chimichurri sauce on the side.

Preparation Tips:
1. If you have time, let the chimichurri sauce sit overnight. In this way the flavors will come together and deepen.
2. Let the ribs rest for a few minutes after grilling. As a result, the meat's juices can be distributed more evenly.

Nutritional Value Per Serving: Calories: 952, Fat: 74.1g, Carbohydrates: 3.2g, Protein: 65.6g

95.   Argentine Grilled Flank Steak with Salsa Criolla

Preparation Time: 2 hours (includes marinating time)
Cooking Time: 15 minutes   **Servings:** 4

Ingredients:
- *Flank Steak - 2 lbs*
- *Salt - to taste*
- *Pepper - to taste*
- *Olive Oil - 2 tbsp*
- *Lemon Juice - from 1 lemon*

For the Salsa Criolla:
- *Red Onion - 1 medium, finely chopped*
- *Red Bell Pepper - 1, finely chopped*
- *Green Bell Pepper - 1, finely chopped*
- *Tomatoes - 2, finely chopped*
- *Parsley - 1/4 cup, finely chopped*
- *Olive Oil - 1/4 cup*
- *White Wine Vinegar - 1/4 cup*
- *Salt - to taste 9.Pepper - to taste*

Directions:
In a bowl, mix together the olive oil and lemon juice. Season the flank steak with salt and pepper, then pour the mixture over the steak. Let it marinate for about 2 hours. Meanwhile, prepare the Salsa Criolla: in a separate bowl, combine chopped onions, red and green bell peppers, tomatoes, parsley, olive oil, white wine vinegar, salt, and pepper. Stir well and refrigerate until ready to serve.

Preheat your grill to high heat.

Shake off any excess marinade before removing the flank steak. Grill the steak for about 5-7 minutes on each side.

Remove the steak from the grill and let it rest for a few minutes. Then, cut the steak against the grain and serve with the Salsa Criolla on the side.

Shopping Tips:
1. For the best flavor, choose a flank steak that is bright red in color, with a bit of marbling.
2. Fresh vegetables are crucial for the Salsa Criolla. Choose ripe tomatoes and crisp peppers for the best results.

Preparation Tips:
1. Slice the vegetables for the Salsa Criolla as finely as possible. The flavors will be able to combine better as a result.
2. Be sure to let your steak rest after grilling before slicing it. This helps the juices redistribute, and result in a juicier steak.

Nutritional Value Per Serving: Calories: 574, Fat: 34.5g, Carbohydrates: 9.6g, Protein: 43.8g

96.   Argentine BBQ Chicken with Malbec BBQ Sauce

Preparation Time: 1 hour (includes marinating time)
Cooking Time: 45 minutes   **Servings:** 4

Ingredients:
- Chicken (whole or parts) - 1, about 3-4 lbs
- Salt - to taste
- Pepper - to taste
- Olive Oil - 2 tbsp
- Lemon Juice - from 1 lemon

For the Malbec BBQ Sauce:
- Olive Oil - 1 tbsp
- Onion - 1, finely chopped
- Garlic Cloves - 4, minced
- Tomato Paste - 1 cup
- Malbec Wine - 1 cup
- Honey - 1/4 cup
- Apple Cider Vinegar - 1/4 cup
- Salt - to taste
- Pepper - to taste

Directions: In a bowl, combine the olive oil and lemon juice. Season the chicken with salt and pepper, then pour the mixture over the chicken. Let it marinate for about 1 hour.
Meanwhile, prepare the Malbec BBQ Sauce: in a saucepan, heat olive oil over medium heat. Add the garlic and onions, sauté until they are soft. Add the tomato paste, Malbec wine, honey, apple cider vinegar, salt, and pepper. Simmer for about 20 minutes, until the sauce has thickened.
Preheat your grill to medium heat.
Remove the chicken from the marinade, discarding any excess. Place the chicken on the grill, skin side down. Grill for about 15 minutes, then flip and grill for another 20-30 minutes. In the last 10 minutes of grilling, coat the chicken with the Malbec BBQ Sauce. Remove the chicken from the grill and let it rest for a few minutes before serving. Enjoy your Argentine BBQ Chicken with the remaining Malbec BBQ Sauce.

Shopping Tips:
1. Choose a chicken that is fresh and of high quality. Organic or free-range chickens generally have a better flavor.
2. Malbec wine is crucial for this recipe. Choose a decent bottle, as the wine's flavor will be pronounced in the sauce.

Preparation Tips:
1. Don't rush the marinating process. Giving the chicken time to marinate will result in a more flavorful dish.
2. Be patient when grilling the chicken. Keeping the grill at medium heat and not rushing the cooking process will result in a juicier, more flavorful chicken.

Nutritional Value Per Serving: Calories: 618, Fat: 33.8g, Carbohydrates: 26.3g, Protein: 38.4g

Japanese Recipes

97.   Yakitori (Japanese Grilled Skewered Chicken)

Preparation Time: 1 hour (includes marinating time)
Cooking Time: 20 minutes   **Servings:** 4

Ingredients:
- Boneless, skin-on chicken thighs - 1.5 lbs
- Green onions/scallions - 8, cut into 1-inch pieces
- Wooden skewers - 12, soaked in water for 30 minutes

For the Yakitori Sauce (Tare):
- Soy sauce - 1/2 cup
- Mirin (Japanese sweet rice wine) - 1/2 cup
- Sake (Japanese rice wine) - 2 tablespoons
- Sugar - 2 tablespoons

Directions: In a saucepan, combine the soy sauce, mirin, sake, and sugar. Bring to a boil, then reduce the heat to low and simmer for about 20 minutes, until the sauce has thickened. Set aside to cool.
Cut the chicken thighs into 1-inch pieces. Thread the chicken pieces and green onions alternately onto the skewers.
Preheat your grill to medium heat. Grill the skewers for about 5 minutes on each side. During the last few minutes of grilling, baste the skewers with the yakitori sauce.
Remove the skewers from the grill and serve with extra yakitori sauce on the side.

Shopping Tips:
1. Choose boneless, skin-on chicken thighs for the juiciness and the best flavor.

Nutritional Value Per Serving: Calories: 374, Fat: 18.6g, Carbohydrates: 22.3g, Protein: 33.4g

---

98.   Tebasaki (Japanese Grilled Chicken Wings)

Preparation Time: 1 hour (includes marinating time)
Cooking Time: 25 minutes   **Servings:** 4

Ingredients:
- Chicken wings - 2 lbs
- Salt - 1 teaspoon
- Pepper - 1/2 teaspoon

For the Tebasaki Sauce:

- *Soy sauce - 1/2 cup*
- *Mirin - 1/2 cup*
- *Sake - 1/4 cup*
- *Sugar - 1/4 cup*
- *Garlic - 2 cloves, minced*
- *Ginger - 1-inch piece, grated*

Directions: In a saucepan, combine the soy sauce, mirin, sake, sugar, garlic, and ginger. Bring to a boil, then reduce the heat to low and simmer for about 20 minutes, until the sauce has thickened. Set aside to cool.

Season the chicken wings with salt and pepper, then marinate them in half of the tebasaki sauce for about 1 hour.

Preheat your grill to medium heat. Grill the chicken wings for about 10-12 minutes on each side, until they are cooked through and the skin is crispy.

During the last few minutes of grilling, baste the chicken wings with the remaining tebasaki sauce. Remove the chicken wings from the grill and serve with extra tebasaki sauce on the side.

Preparation Tips:
1. Marinating the chicken wings in the sauce not only adds flavor but also helps to achieve a glaze-like finish when grilling.

Nutritional Value Per Serving: Calories: 403, Fat: 28.6g, Carbohydrates: 19.4g, Protein: 21.3g

99.   Yuzu Kosho Chicken

Preparation Time: 2 hours (includes marinating time)
Cooking Time: 20 minutes   **Servings:** 4

Ingredients:
- *Chicken thighs - 2 lbs*
- *Salt - 1 teaspoon*
- *Pepper - 1/2 teaspoon*

For the Yuzu Kosho Marinade:
- *Yuzu Kosho - 2 tablespoons*
- *Soy Sauce - 2 tablespoons*
- *Mirin - 2 tablespoons*
- *Sesame oil - 1 tablespoon*
- *Garlic - 2 cloves, minced*
- *Ginger - 1-inch piece, grated*

Directions: In a bowl, combine the yuzu kosho, soy sauce, mirin, sesame oil, garlic, and ginger to make the marinade.

Season the chicken thighs with salt and pepper, then marinate them in the yuzu kosho mixture for about 2 hours.

Preheat your grill to medium heat. Grill the chicken thighs for about 10 minutes on each side, until they are cooked through and have a nice char.

Remove the chicken thighs from the grill and let them rest for a few minutes before serving.

Shopping Tips:
1. Yuzu kosho is a spicy Japanese condiment made from yuzu (a type of citrus), chili peppers, and salt.

Preparation Tips:
1. Letting the chicken marinate for 2 hours will allow the meat to absorb the flavors completely.

Nutritional Value Per Serving: Calories: 461, Fat: 28.7g, Carbohydrates: 8.8g, Protein: 43.2g

Mediterranean and Greek Recipes

100.   Mediterranean Grilled Shrimp Skewers

Preparation Time: 45 minutes (includes marinating time)
Cooking Time: 10 minutes   **Servings:** 4

Ingredients:
- Large shrimp, peeled and deveined - 2 lbs
- Lemon - 2, zest and juice
- Olive oil - 1/4 cup
- Garlic - 4 cloves, minced
- Fresh parsley - 2 tablespoons, chopped
- Paprika - 1 teaspoon
- Salt - 1 teaspoon
- Pepper - 1/2 teaspoon
- Wooden skewers - 12, soaked in water for 30 minutes

Directions: In a bowl, combine the lemon zest, lemon juice, olive oil, garlic, parsley, paprika, salt, and pepper. Add the shrimp and toss to coat. Cover and refrigerate for 30 minutes to marinate.

Preheat your grill to medium-high heat. Thread the shrimp onto the skewers.

Grill the skewers for 2-3 minutes on each side.

Remove the skewers from the grill and serve with fresh lemon wedges.

Shopping Tips:
1. Choose large, fresh shrimp for the best flavor and texture.

Nutritional Value Per Serving: Calories: 287, Fat: 11.3g, Carbohydrates: 8.3g, Protein: 41.8g

101. Mediterranean Grilled Swordfish Steaks

Preparation Time: 30 minutes (includes marinating time)
Cooking Time: 10 minutes   **Servings:** 4

Ingredients:

- Swordfish steaks - 4 (6-ounce each)
- Olive oil - 1/4 cup
- Lemon - 2, juice and zest
- Fresh rosemary - 2 tablespoons, chopped
- Garlic - 4 cloves, minced
- Salt - 1 teaspoon
- Pepper - 1/2 teaspoon

Directions: In a bowl, combine the olive oil, lemon juice, lemon zest, rosemary, garlic, salt, and pepper. Add the steaks, then stir to coat. Cover and refrigerate for 30 minutes to marinate.
Preheat your grill to medium-high heat. Place the swordfish on the grill after removing it from the marinade.
Grill the swordfish for 4-5 minutes on each side.
Remove the swordfish from the grill and serve with fresh lemon wedges.

Shopping Tips:

1. Look for fresh swordfish steaks that are firm to the touch and have a slight pink hue.

Preparation Tips:

1. Marinating the swordfish in a lemon and rosemary marinade not only adds flavor but also helps to keep the fish moist while grilling.

Nutritional Value Per Serving: Calories: 322, Fat: 14.6g, Carbohydrates: 5.3g, Protein: 40.6g

---

102. Mediterranean Grilled Octopus

Preparation Time: 4 hours (includes marinating time)
Cooking Time: 15 minutes   **Servings:** 4

Ingredients:

- Octopus - 2 lbs, cleaned and cut into pieces
- Olive oil - 1/4 cup
- Red wine vinegar - 2 tablespoons
- Garlic - 4 cloves, minced
- Oregano - 2 teaspoons, dried
- Lemon - 2, juice and zest
- Salt - 1 teaspoon

- *Pepper - 1/2 teaspoon*
- *Fresh parsley - for garnish*

Directions: In a bowl, combine the olive oil, red wine vinegar, garlic, oregano, lemon juice, lemon zest, salt, and pepper. Add the octopus and toss to coat. Cover and refrigerate for at least 3 hours to marinate.

Preheat your grill to medium-high heat. Remove the octopus from the marinade and place on the grill.

Grill the octopus for about 7-8 minutes on each side.

Remove the octopus from the grill, garnish with fresh parsley and serve with fresh lemon wedges.

Shopping Tips:
1. Look for fresh octopus at your local fish market. If you can only find frozen, thaw it in the refrigerator overnight before marinating.

Preparation Tips:
1. Marinating the octopus in a lemon and oregano marinade enhances the flavor and helps to tenderize the meat.

Nutritional Value Per Serving: Calories: 319, ì Fat: 14.6g, Carbohydrates: 8.3g, Protein: 34.5g

---

103.   Greek-Style Grilled Pork Chops with Tzatziki

Preparation Time: 1 hour (includes marinating time)
Cooking Time: 15 minutes   **Servings:** 4

Ingredients:
- *Pork chops - 4 (6-ounce each, bone-in)*
- *Olive oil - 1/4 cup*
- *Lemon - 2, juice and zest*
- *Fresh oregano - 2 tablespoons, chopped*
- *Garlic - 4 cloves, minced*
- *Salt - 1 teaspoon*
- *Pepper - 1/2 teaspoon*
- *Tzatziki sauce - to serve*
- *Fresh dill - for garnish*

Directions: In a bowl, combine the olive oil, lemon juice, lemon zest, oregano, garlic, salt, and pepper. Add the pork chops and turn to coat. Cover and refrigerate for 1 hour to marinate.

Preheat your grill to medium-high heat. Remove the pork chops from the marinade and place on the grill.

Grill the pork chops for 6-7 minutes on each side, until the internal temperature reaches 145 degrees F on a meat thermometer.

Remove the pork chops from the grill, allow them to rest for a few minutes. Garnish with fresh dill and serve with tzatziki sauce.

Shopping Tips:
1. Look for fresh, bone-in pork chops for the best flavor and moisture retention.

Preparation Tips:
1. Marinating the pork chops in a lemon and oregano marinade not only adds Greek flavor but also helps to keep the meat tender and juicy while grilling.

Nutritional Value Per Serving: Calories: 334, Fat: 16.6g, Carbohydrates: 3.4g, Protein: 41.6g

---

104.   Greek Souvlaki Pork Skewers

Preparation Time: 1 hour (includes marinating time)
Cooking Time: 15 minutes   **Servings:** 4

Ingredients:
- Pork shoulder - 2 lbs, cut into 1-inch cubes
- Olive oil - 1/4 cup
- Lemon - 2, juice and zest
- Fresh oregano - 2 tablespoons, chopped
- Garlic - 4 cloves, minced
- Salt - 1 teaspoon
- Pepper - 1/2 teaspoon
- Wooden skewers - 8, soaked in water for 30 minutes
- Tzatziki sauce - to serve

Directions:
In a bowl, combine the lemon zest, olive oil, oregano, lemon juice, garlic, salt, and pepper. Add the pork cubes and toss to coat. Cover and refrigerate for 1 hour to marinate.
Preheat your grill to medium-high heat. Thread the pork onto the skewers.
Grill the skewers for 6-7 minutes on each side.
Remove the skewers from the grill and serve with tzatziki sauce.

Shopping Tips:
1. Choose a well-marbled cut of pork, such as the shoulder, for the best flavor and moisture.

Nutritional Value Per Serving: Calories: 468, Fat: 32.7g, Carbohydrates: 3.3g, Protein: 37.5g

105. Grilled Pork Souvlaki Pitas

Preparation Time: 1 hour (includes marinating time)
Cooking Time: 15 minutes   **Servings:** 4

Ingredients:
- Pork tenderloin - 1.5 lbs, cut into 1-inch cubes
- Olive oil - 1/4 cup
- Lemon - 2, juice and zest
- Fresh oregano - 2 tablespoons, chopped
- Garlic - 4 cloves, minced
- Salt - 1 teaspoon
- Pepper - 1/2 teaspoon
- Pita bread - 4 pieces
- Tzatziki sauce - to serve
- Sliced tomatoes, cucumbers, and onions - for garnish

Directions: In a bowl, combine the olive oil, lemon juice, lemon zest, oregano, garlic, salt, and pepper. Add the pork cubes and toss to coat. Cover and refrigerate for 1 hour to marinate.
Preheat your grill to medium-high heat. Thread the pork onto the skewers.
Grill the skewers for 6-7 minutes on each side.
Grill the pita bread for about 1 minute on each side, until lightly toasted.
Remove the skewers and pitas from the grill. Slide the pork off the skewers into the pita bread, top with tzatziki sauce, tomatoes, cucumbers, and onions.

Shopping Tips:
1. Pork tenderloin is a lean cut that's ideal for grilling. It's also conveniently sized for skewering and cooking quickly on the grill.

Preparation Tips:
1. Using pita bread as a vessel for your grilled pork adds a nice textural contrast and makes for a more substantial, handheld meal.

Nutritional Value Per Serving: Calories: 463, Fat: 13.5g, Carbohydrates: 36.1g, Protein: 46.2g

Kebabs

106.   Persian Joojeh (Chicken) Kebab

Preparation Time: 2 hours (includes marinating time)
Cooking Time: 10-15 minutes   **Servings:** 4

Ingredients:

- Boneless skinless chicken breasts - 1.5 lbs, cut into 1-inch cubes
- Plain yogurt - 1 cup
- Lemon - 1, juice and zest
- Saffron - 1 teaspoon, crushed and soaked in 2 tablespoons of hot water
- Garlic - 3 cloves, minced
- Salt - 1 teaspoon
- Pepper - 1/2 teaspoon
- Olive oil - 1 tablespoon
- Flat metal skewers - 4

Directions: In a bowl, mix the yogurt, lemon juice, lemon zest, saffron water, garlic, salt, pepper, and olive oil. Add the chicken cubes, toss to coat, cover, and refrigerate for at least 2 hours, or overnight.

Preheat your grill to medium-high heat. Thread the chicken onto the skewers with some space between each piece.

Grill the skewers for 4-5 minutes on each side.

Remove the skewers from the grill and serve with grilled tomatoes and basmati rice.

Shopping Tips:

1. Look for high-quality, fresh chicken breasts. Organic, free-range options typically have the best flavor.

Preparation Tips:

1. Marinating the chicken in a yogurt and saffron marinade enhances the Persian flavor and helps to tenderize and juicy the meat while grilling.

Nutritional Value Per Serving: Calories: 297, Fat: 8.3g, Carbohydrates: 4.2g, Protein: 48.9g

107. Turkish Lamb Adana Kebab

Preparation Time: 2 hours (includes resting time)
Cooking Time: 10-15 minutes   **Servings:** 4

Ingredients:
- Ground lamb - 1.5 lbs
- Red bell pepper - 1, finely chopped
- Onion - 1 medium, finely chopped
- Garlic - 3 cloves, minced
- Paprika - 2 teaspoons
- Cumin - 1 teaspoon
- Salt - 1 teaspoon
- Black pepper - 1/2 teaspoon
- Flat metal skewers - 4

Directions:
In a bowl, combine the ground lamb, bell pepper, onion, garlic, paprika, cumin, salt, and black pepper. Knead until everything is well combined.
Divide the mixture into 4 equal parts and mold each around the length of a skewer, flattening into a sausage shape. Cover and refrigerate for at least 2 hours to firm up. Preheat your grill to medium-high heat. Grill the skewers for 5-7 minutes on each side. Remove the skewers from the grill and serve with flatbread, fresh parsley, and sumac onions.

Shopping Tips:
1. For the most flavorful results, choose ground lamb that's not too lean. A little bit of fat will make your kebabs juicier.

Preparation Tips:
1. When shaping the lamb around the skewers, ensure the meat is evenly distributed for balanced grilling.

Nutritional Value Per Serving: Calories: 353, ì Fat: 24.2g, Carbohydrates: 6.3g, Protein: 28.4g

108.   Indian Style Paneer Tikka Kebab

Preparation Time: 2 hours (includes marinating time)
Cooking Time: 10-15 minutes   **Servings:** 4

Ingredients:

- *Paneer - 1.5 lbs, cut into 1-inch cubes*
- *Greek yogurt - 1 cup*
- *Lemon - 1, juice and zest*
- *Garam masala - 2 teaspoons*
- *Turmeric - 1 teaspoon*
- *Chili powder - 1 teaspoon*
- *Garlic - 3 cloves, minced*
- *Salt - 1 teaspoon*
- *Olive oil - 1 tablespoon*
- *Onion - 1, cut into 1-inch pieces*
- *Bell pepper - 1, cut into 1-inch pieces*
- *Flat metal skewers - 4*

Directions: In a bowl, mix the yogurt, lemon juice, lemon zest, garam masala, turmeric, chili powder, garlic, salt, and olive oil. Add the paneer, onion, and bell pepper, toss to coat, cover, and refrigerate for at least 2 hours.

Preheat your grill to medium-high heat. Thread the paneer, onion, and bell pepper onto the skewers, alternating between each.

Grill the skewers for 4-5 minutes on each side, until the paneer is lightly charred and the vegetables are tender.

Remove the skewers from the grill and serve with naan and mint chutney.

Shopping Tips:

1. Paneer is a type of Indian cheese that holds its shape when cooked, making it perfect for grilling.

Preparation Tips:

1. Paneer doesn't melt like many cheeses, so you can grill it directly without worrying about it falling through the grates.

Nutritional Value Per Serving: Calories: 358, Fat: 24.3g, Carbohydrates: 11.6g, Protein: 23.5g

Appendix

Grill Terminology

1. **Asado**: A South American grilling technique involving slow-cooking meat over a wood-fired grill.

2. **Bark**: The dark, flavorful crust that forms on meat (usually pork or beef) during long, slow cooking.

3. **Basting**: Applying juices, sauces, or marinades to food while it is cooking, typically using a brush or spoon.

4. **BBQ**: An abbreviation for "barbecue", a method of cooking food over an open fire or on a grill.

5. **BBQ Tongs**: A tool used for turning or lifting food on the grill. BBQ tongs should be long enough to maintain a safe distance between your hands and the heat.

6. **Briquette**: A lump of tightly compressed coal dust or charcoal used as fuel for a BBQ grill.

7. **Char**: To burn or reduce food to carbon, creating a blackened exterior.

8. **Chimney Starter**: A device used to ignite charcoal briquettes or hardwood charcoal.

9. **Cold Smoking**: A method of preserving and flavoring food, particularly meat and fish, by exposing it to the smoke from a controlled source of heat.

10. **Direct Grilling**: A grilling method where food is grilled over the heat source directly.

11. **Dirty Steak**: A method of cooking steak by placing it directly on the coals of your grill.

12. **Drip Pan**: A pan placed under food being grilled to catch drippings, which can be used for basting or making sauce.

13. **Dry Rub**: A blend of dry herbs and spices rubbed onto meat before grilling to add flavor.

14. **Fish Basket**: A flat, hinged basket designed to hold fish. It keeps the fish intact while grilling and makes turning easier.

15. **Grill Basket**: A tool that holds foods (often delicate or small items) so they don't fall through the grill grates.

16. **Grill Brush:** A tool used to clean the surface of the grill. It often features a long handle and hard, wire bristles.

17. **Grill Fork:** A long, two-pronged fork used for turning and testing the doneness of meat. It should be used sparingly to avoid juice loss from the meat.

18. **Grill Grates:** The surface on which the food is cooked. They can be made of several different materials, including cast iron and stainless steel.

19. **Grill Marks**: The aesthetically pleasing lines created on the surface of food from the grill grates when seared correctly.

20. **Grill Press:** A flat weight with a handle used to press food down onto the grill, promoting even cooking and nice grill marks.

21. **Grill Spatula:** A flat utensil used to flip burgers and other foods. Grill spatulas should be sturdy and heat-resistant.

22. **Indirect Grilling**: A grilling method where food is cooked away from the heat source, typically used for foods that require longer cooking times or larger chunks of meat.

23. **Infra-Red Burner**: A burner that uses infra-red energy to heat food on a grill, often used in high-end gas grills.

24. **Instant-Read Thermometer**: A device used to quickly measure the temperature of food. It's crucial for ensuring meat is cooked to the proper internal temperature.

25. **Kebab**: Skewered chunks of meat (and sometimes vegetables) cooked on a grill.

26. **Marinade**: A sauce, typically made of oil, herbs, spices, and vinegar in which fish, meat, or other foods are soaked before cooking to season or tenderize them.

27. **Meat Injector**: A syringe-like tool used to inject liquids, such as marinades or melted butter, directly into meat for additional flavor.

28. **Pitmaster**: A person who runs a barbecue. Sometimes, in the case of competitions, this person might be a chef responsible for all menu planning, prep, and cooking.

29. **Pizza Stone**: A flat stone or piece of ceramic used to evenly distribute heat and absorb moisture, resulting in a crisp crust.

30. **Planking**: A method of grilling where food is placed on a wooden plank, adding unique flavors to the food.

31. **Pull Temperature**: The internal temperature at which you should remove your meat from the grill, considering that the temperature will continue to rise as the meat rests.

32. **Reverse Sear**: A technique where you cook your meat over very low indirect heat before searing it over high direct heat.

33. **Rib Rack**: A metal rack that can be used to roast many racks of ribs simultaneously. It also promotes even cooking and easy basting.

34. **Rotisserie**: A method of cooking where meat is held on a long rod called a spit as it is cooked over a fire or in an oven.

35. **Sear**: To make the meat's outside brown by short, high-heat exposure, locking in the juices.

36. **Smoking**: A method of cooking where food, commonly meat or fish, is exposed to the smoke from a controlled source of heat. The food absorbs the smoke flavor.

37. **Snake Method**: A charcoal arrangement technique where briquettes are lined up in a row, forming a snake-like shape. This method allows for long, slow, indirect cooking.

38. **Tandoor**: A cylindrical clay oven for baking and cooking. It operates by creating a hot, smoky fire at the bottom of the drum.

39. **Veggie Basket**: A grill tool with small holes that allow heat and smoke to reach the vegetables while being kept from dropping through the grates.

40. **Water Smoker:** A type of smoker that uses water to keep the temperature low and stable, and to add humidity, preventing the food from drying out.

41. **Wet Rub:** A mixture of herbs and spices plus a wet ingredient such as oil, vinegar, or yogurt.

42. **Wok Topper**: A grill accessory that allows you to cook small or delicate foods on the grill that would otherwise fall through the grates.

43. **Wood Chips**: Small pieces of hardwood that are soaked in water and added to a charcoal or gas grill for smoke flavor.

44. **Yakitori**: Japanese skewered chicken, cooked on a grill with either sweet soy sauce or salt.

45. **Zone Cooking (or Two-Zone Grilling)**: A technique that involves creating two areas on your grill, one for high, direct heat and another for lower, indirect heat. This method gives you the flexibility to sear food over high heat and then move it to lower heat to finish cooking.

The Most Popular Types of Grills

1. **Built-In or Drop-In Grills:** These are permanent grills that are built into outdoor kitchens. They can run on gas or charcoal and are often large, allowing for bigger cookouts.

2. **Charcoal Grills**: Known for the smoky flavor they impart, charcoal grills require the use of charcoal briquettes or lump charcoal as fuel. They require more time for preheating and cleanup compared to other grills.

3. **Electric Grills:** Ideal for residents of condos and apartments where charcoal and gas grills are prohibited. They plug into an electrical outlet and cook food using heated grill plates. No smoke or flames are produced.

4. **Gas Grills**: These grills use natural gas or propane as fuel. They heat up quickly, making them convenient for weeknight cooking. Some models have side burners for cooking side dishes and sauces.

5. **Infrared Grills:** These use a gas or electric heat source to heat a solid surface that then emits infrared waves that cook the food. They are known for their ability to evenly spread heat and minimize flare-ups.

6. **Kamado Grills:** Made from ceramic material, Kamado grills are excellent for holding heat. They use charcoal as fuel and can be used for smoking, grilling, roasting, and baking pizzas. The most famous brand is the "Big Green Egg."

7. **Pellet Grills:** These grills use wood pellets as fuel and a fan to circulate heat and smoke in the grill. They are versatile and can grill, smoke, roast, and even bake.

8. **Portable Grills**: These are available in gas, charcoal, or electric versions. They are ideal for tailgating, camping, and picnics because they are lightweight, small, and portable.

9. **Rotisserie Grills**: These grills have a rotating spit where the food, commonly whole chickens or roasts, is impaled and then slowly rotated over the heat source for even cooking.

10. **Smokers**: While technically not a grill, smokers are outdoor cooking appliances that are used to smoke meats over long periods. They can use wood, charcoal, or gas as fuel, and the smoke gives the food a unique, robust flavor.

Recipes Index

Greek-Style Grilled Lamb Kebabs	42
Greek-Style Grilled Pork Chops with Tzatziki	94
Grilled Apple Crisp Foil Packets	85
Grilled Artichokes with Garlic-Lemon Aioli	70
Grilled Asparagus with Lemon and Parmesan	68
Grilled Banana Split	83
Grilled Beef Kebabs with Vegetables	35
Grilled Beef Sliders with BBQ Sauce	41
Grilled Berries with Sweet Cream	84
Grilled Cherry Clafoutis	85
Grilled Chicken Alfredo Pizza	48
Grilled Chicken Caesar Salad	47
Grilled Chicken Parmesan	50
Grilled Chicken Quesadillas	48
Grilled Chicken Skewers with Peanut Sauce	49
Grilled Chicken Tacos with Mango Salsa	49
Grilled Clams with Herb Butter	64
Grilled Corn on the Cob with Garlic Herb Butter	67
Grilled Eggplant with Tomato and Feta	70
Grilled Lamb Chops with Rosemary and Garlic	41
Grilled Lamb Leg with Lemon and Oregano	43
Grilled Lemon-Pepper Tuna Steaks	61
Grilled Lobster Tails with Garlic Butter	63
Grilled Mahi Mahi with Mango Salsa	61
Grilled Mussels with Garlic-Lemon Butter	65
Grilled Oysters with Spicy Butter	64
Grilled Peaches with Vanilla Ice Cream	83
Grilled Pineapple with Honey-Cinnamon Glaze	82
Grilled Pork Skewers with Pineapple Salsa	56
Grilled Pork Souvlaki Pitas	96
Grilled Pork Tenderloin with Herb Rub	55
Grilled Pork Tenderloin with Peach Glaze	57
Grilled Pork Tenderloin with Pineapple Salsa	58
Grilled Portobello Mushrooms with Balsamic Glaze	67
Grilled Scallops with Lemon Herb Sauce	63
Grilled Shrimp Skewers with Garlic-Lime Marinade	62
Grilled Skirt Steak with Chimichurri Sauce	33
Grilled Strawberry Shortcake Kebabs	86
Grilled Swordfish with Herb Butter	62
Grilled T-Bone Steaks with BBQ Rub	34

Grilled T-Bone Steaks with Garlic Herb Butter	34
Grilled Turkey Burgers with Avocado	51
Grilled Zucchini Ribbons with Pesto and Pine Nuts	69
Grilled Zucchini with Parmesan	66

H

Herb and Garlic Rub	74
Herb Grilled Turkey Breast	51
Herb Marinade	80
Honey BBQ Chicken Wings	45
Honey Garlic Pork Chops	56
Honey Lime Grilled Salmon	60
Honey Mustard Grilled Chicken Salad	50
Honey Mustard Sauce	75
Honey Mustard Sauce	77

I

Indian Style Paneer Tikka Kebab	99

L

Lamb Burger with Mint and Feta	42
Lemon and Garlic Grilled Turkey Cutlets	52
Lemon-Garlic Marinade	79
Lemon-Pepper Rub	73

M

Maple-Glazed Butternut Squash	71
Mediterranean Grilled Shrimp Skewers	92
Mediterranean Grilled Swordfish Steaks	93

P

Persian Joojeh (Chicken) Kebab	97

S

Savory Rib-Eye Steak with Herb Butter	31
Smoky BBQ Beef Brisket	30
Smoky BBQ Beef Skewers	37
Spicy Asian Marinade	80
Spicy BBQ Beef Kebabs	39
Spicy BBQ Sauce	76
Spicy BBQ Sauce	77

Made in the USA
Coppell, TX
21 February 2024

29249973R00059